MARTIN McDONAGH

The Lonesome West

with commentary and notes by
PATRICK LONERGAN

METHUEN DRAMA

Methuen Drama Student Edition

Methuen Drama, an imprint of Bloomsbury Publishing Plc

10 9 8 7 6 5 4 3

This edition first published in the United Kingdom in 2010 by
Methuen Drama
Bloomsbury Publishing Plc
50 Bedford Square
London WC1B 3DP
www.methuendrama.com

The Lonesome West first published in 1997 by Methuen Drama in
association with the Royal Court Theatre
Copyright © 1997 by Martin McDonagh

Commentary and notes copyright © 2010 by Methuen Drama

ISBN 978 1 408 12576 2

A CIP catalogue record for this book is available from the British Library

Available in the USA from Bloomsbury Academic & Professional, 175
Fith Avenue/3rd Floor, New York, NY 10010.
www.BloomsburyAcademicUSA.com

Typeset by SX Composing DTP, Rayleigh, Essex
Printed by CPI Group (UK) Ltd, Croydon CR0 4YY

Contents

Thanks to Sinead McPhillips of Druid Theatre for providing access to a DVD of the original production of *The Lonesome West*; to Vera Orschel for facilitating access to the Druid archive at National University of Ireland, Galway; and to Shelley Troupe for research assistance. Some of the research presented in this book was carried out as part of a project on Irish drama which is being funded by the Irish Research Council for the Humanities and Social Sciences.

P.L.

Martin McDonagh

1970 On 26 March, Martin McDonagh is born in south-east London. His father, John, is originally from Connemara, while his mother Mary McDonagh (*née* Harte) is originally from Sligo. With his elder brother John Michael, McDonagh will spend many summer holidays during his childhood returning to the west of Ireland to visit his parents' families.

1984 McDonagh's first visit to the theatre, to see Al Pacino playing Don in David Mamet's *American Buffalo*, at the Duke of York's Theatre, London. During the next thirteen years, McDonagh only goes to the theatre occasionally: he states in 1997 that he has seen 'maybe twenty plays'.

1986–93 McDonagh quits school at the age of sixteen. He works in a variety of jobs during this period, stocking shelves at a supermarket and doing clerical work at the Department of Trade and Industry. He also spends some time on the dole, receiving social welfare payments. He begins writing during the early 1990s. His parents return to Ireland, while he and his brother remain in London, both spending most of their time writing.

1994 Realising that his style is too obviously influenced by the work of Mamet and Harold Pinter, McDonagh decides to start writing in an exaggerated version of the speech he has heard during summer visits to Ireland. This inspires a burst of creativity and he drafts seven plays in quick succession: *The Beauty Queen of Leenane*, *A Skull in Connemara* and *The Lonesome West* (collectively known as *The Leenane Trilogy*); *The Cripple of Inishmaan*, *The Lieutenant of Inishmore* and *The*

Banshees of Inisheer (collectively known as *The Aran Islands Trilogy*); and *The Pillowman*. Six of these plays will be produced between 1996 and 2003.

1995   Garry Hynes, who has recently returned to Galway's Druid Theatre after working as artistic director of the Abbey Theatre in Dublin, decides to read through the company's recent batch of unsolicited submissions. She finds McDonagh's scripts and immediately buys the rights to stage three of them.

1996   Druid Theatre premieres *The Beauty Queen of Leenane* at the Town Hall Theatre on 1 February. Garry Hynes directs. After a brief Irish tour, it transfers to the Royal Court Theatre Upstairs, opening on 29 February. In November, the play opens at the Duke of York's Theatre in London's West End. As the year concludes, McDonagh is named 'Most Promising Newcomer' at the George Devine Awards. A confrontation with Sean Connery at the awards ceremony is widely reported.

1997   *The Cripple of Inishmaan* opens at the Royal National Theatre in January, where it is directed by Nicholas Hytner. In April, a rehearsed reading of *The Pillowman* is staged in Galway as part of the Cúirt International Festival of Literature. In June, *A Skull in Connemara* and *The Lonesome West* premiere in Galway, where they play in repertory with *The Beauty Queen* as *The Leenane Trilogy*, which is again directed by Hynes. The *Trilogy* transfers to the Royal Court in London in July.

1998   *The Leenane Trilogy* tours in January to the Sydney Festival. In April, *The Beauty Queen* opens at the Walter Kerr Theater in New York. It is nominated for six Tony Awards, winning four of them. Hynes becomes the first woman to win a Tony for direction. In November, *The Lonesome West* tours rural Ireland in a production that stars Jon Kenny and Pat Shortt – better known in Ireland as the comedy duo The D'Unbelievables.

1999   On 27 April, *The Lonesome West* opens at the Lyceum
Theater on Broadway, where it is nominated for
four Tonys. McDonagh's attempts to produce *The
Lieutenant of Inishmore* are unsuccessful; he declares
that he will not produce any more plays until *The
Lieutenant* appears.

2000   Druid's production of *The Beauty Queen* receives an
extended run in Dublin for the first time, playing at
the Gaiety Theatre for almost three months during
the year. While it is a commercial success, Dublin
reviewers are generally critical of what they see as
the production's 'stage Irish' qualities.

2001   *The Lieutenant of Inishmore* is premiered by the Royal
Shakespeare Company at the Other Place,
Stratford-upon-Avon, directed by Wilson Milam. It
transfers to the Barbican in London later that year.
The Lonesome West receives its first extended run in
Dublin, playing from 2 August to 29 September.

2002   *The Lieutenant of Inishmore* plays at the Garrick
Theatre in London's West End. It wins an Olivier
Award for Best New Comedy.

2003   In October, John Crowley directs the premiere of
The Pillowman at the Royal National Theatre.

2004   *The Pillowman* wins an Olivier Award for Best New
Play.

2005   McDonagh writes and directs a short film, *Six
Shooter*. The RNT's production of *The Pillowman* visits
Ireland, playing for five nights in Cork in March.
The following month, *The Pillowman* opens at the
Booth Theater on Broadway, in a production
directed by John Crowley that stars Jeff Goldblum
and Billy Crudup. It is nominated for four Tonys,
winning two (for set and lighting design). The first
major Irish revival of *The Lonesome West* takes place.
Co-produced by An Grianán Theatre Donegal and
the Lyric Theatre Belfast, the production tours
Ireland from September to November.

2006   McDonagh wins an Oscar for best short film for *Six
Shooter*. Wilson Milam's production of *The Lieutenant*

of Inishmore opens at New York's Atlantic Theater in February. It transfers to Broadway in May, where it is nominated for five Tonys.

2008   McDonagh writes and directs *In Bruges*, his first feature film. Starring Colin Farrell, Brendan Gleeson and Ralph Fiennes, the film is a critical and commercial success. In September, Druid Theatre presents the first professional Irish production of *The Cripple of Inishmaan*, which transfers to New York's Atlantic Theater in December.

2009   McDonagh receives his second Oscar nomination, for Best Original Screenplay for *In Bruges*. Colin Farrell is awarded a Golden Globe for his performance in that film.

2010   McDonagh's seventh play, *A Behanding in Spokane*, premieres on Broadway on 8 March. Directed by John Crowley and starring Christopher Walken, it is the first of McDonagh's plays to be set entirely in America.

Plot

Scene One

The action begins in a rundown farmhouse in rural Galway.
This is the home of Valene and Coleman Connor, two
middle-aged bachelors. The furniture in their living-room
room is tatty and functional: there is a table with two chairs,
a pair of armchairs, some shelves, and little else. Yet the
room also contains many objects that will prove significant
as events unfold. A photograph of Valene's pet dog sits on
the chest of drawers and there are several religious figurines
displayed on shelves. Hanging on the wall at the centre of
the stage are a gun and crucifix, representing the play's
intertwined themes of violence and religion. Almost
everything that we see has been marked with the letter 'V'
to signify that it belongs to Valene.

We soon learn that the funeral of the Connors' father
has just concluded. He was shot dead by Coleman –
accidentally, the brothers claim. Coleman and the local
priest Father Welsh have entered the house. Coleman
grudgingly gives Welsh a drink of poteen as thanks for
saying the funeral mass, making obvious that he has little
respect for the priest. Welsh defends himself against the
accusation that he is an alcoholic, but does so without much
conviction. Valene then enters, and reveals why he has
arrived later than his brother: he had stopped on his way
home to purchase yet another religious figurine, which he
will mark with a letter 'V' and place on a shelf with the rest
of his collection.

We soon understand why Welsh seems so dependent on
alcohol: the behaviour of his parishioners is thoroughly
immoral, and he feels powerless to do anything to improve
matters. His mood is not helped by the actions of the
brothers, who bicker violently with each other. Their
arguments are briefly interrupted by the arrival of Girleen

Kelleher, a seventeen-year-old schoolgirl who is travelling
from house to house, selling poteen. Our first impressions of
Girleen may prove misleading. She ignores the brothers'
news that they have just buried their father, seeming more
interested in talking about the local postman's desire to 'get
into her knickers'. Her reaction when Valene attempts to
pay her less than the agreed price for her poteen reveals that
she is assertive and strong-willed. Girleen has also delivered
a letter on the postman's behalf to Valene: it contains a
large cheque which he has received as a result of his father's
death. He taunts his brother, and the duo start to fight.

By now quite drunk, Father Welsh finally decides that he
can bear no more of such company, and leaves. Girleen
follows him, claiming to be concerned for his welfare, and
the two brothers agree that the priest is far too sensitive.

Scene Two
An enormous orange stove with the letter 'V' scrawled on its
front has appeared stage left. It appears that Valene has
bought it for no reason other than to annoy his brother. As
Coleman will point out during the scene, Valene never eats
anything more substantial than crisps, so he has no need to
cook food.

As the scene begins, Coleman is seated in an armchair,
sipping a glass of poteen and reading one of Valene's
women's magazines. Valene returns and checks the
temperature of the stove: he's obviously hoping to catch
Coleman using it. The two bicker about a variety of inane
subjects, such as the merits of different crisp brands.
Suddenly Valene notices that Coleman is drinking poteen.
He knows that Coleman has no money, so only two
possibilities exist. Either Coleman has stolen some of
Valene's poteen – or he has stolen Valene's house-insurance
money, and used it to buy poteen of his own.

Coleman's explanation is rather incredible: he was given
a bottle of poteen by Girleen, he claims, as payment for
allowing her to grope him. Valene isn't sure whether to
believe this story, but his attention is distracted when

Coleman takes one of his packets of crisps without asking. The appalled Valene demands to be paid for them. This dispute soon breaks into violence – but the brothers are prevented from harming each other too severely by the arrival of Father Welsh, who bursts through the door to reveal that the local policeman, Tom Hanlon, has drowned himself.

The brothers are shocked by this news – but seem much more concerned by another revelation from Welsh: that Girleen had spent the day helping him wash the strips for the local under-twelves football team. This means that Coleman had been lying when he claimed to have been with Girleen earlier that day. Humiliated, Coleman flees to his room.

Father Welsh asks the pair to help him to carry Hanlon's body from the lakeside to his family home, but only Valene agrees to do so. After he and Welsh leave, Coleman returns to the living-room and turns the stove up to its maximum setting. He then gathers all the religious figurines together and places them in a bowl, which he puts in the stove before leaving the house.

Scene Three

Valene and Welsh have returned from Hanlon's home, where they witnessed the agony of his family. Their conversation ranges over a number of topics. They note that Tom and his brother must have loved each other, despite seeming unable to get along – an observation that will later inspire Father Welsh's attempts to redeem Valene and Coleman. And Welsh talks at length about suicide: about the depth of despair that must give rise to the decision to end one's life, and about the Catholic Church's harsh attitude towards those who commit that 'sin'.

Suddenly Valene notices that all his religious figurines are missing; he rushes to the stove and is horrified to find that they have been melted down. He takes the bowl of molten plastic from the stove and places it on the table centre stage while smoke fills the room. In a state of dreadful fury,

Valene grabs the rifle from the wall and declares his intention to shoot his brother. Welsh pleads with him to reconsider, but his words only have the effect of provoking Valene to reveal that his father's death was not an accident: Coleman had shot their father for laughing at his hairstyle. Welsh is devastated by this announcement.

It is at this moment that Coleman chooses to make his entrance. He confirms Valene's revelation and says that Valene had agreed to pretend that the murder was an accident on the condition that he would inherit his father's entire estate. Valene attempts to shoot his brother, but Coleman had taken the precaution of removing the bullets from the gun before his departure earlier. The two begin to fight, rolling around the floor and punching each other. In despair, Welsh places his hands into the bowl of steaming plastic, burning himself dreadfully. He screams in agony and runs from the house. The two brothers are so shocked that they stop fighting; Coleman exits to his own room, and the scene concludes with the confused-looking Valene standing centre stage, scratching his balls.

Scene Four

Father Welsh is sitting alone beside the lake, his hands heavily bandaged. He takes a sip from his pint of stout, and is joined by Girleen. Both have just come from the funeral of Tom Hanlon. Girleen praises Welsh's sermon at the funeral mass, but he doesn't seem to believe her claim that she found his words moving. He is then shocked to learn that Girleen knew the truth about Valene and Coleman's father – and that she also was aware of other murders in Leenane, but had done nothing to bring the killers to justice. Welsh asks Girleen to deliver a letter from him to the brothers.

The pair share a tender moment, as Welsh informs her that he intends to leave Leenane for ever. He pleads with her to stop selling poteen, and the two discuss their given names: Welsh's first name is Roderick and Girleen is really called Mary. The couple's willingness to reveal this personal information may suggest that they could have had a loving relationship with each other.

The conversation then turns to suicide: Girleen declares that it's better to be living than dead because she believes that, regardless of how things seem, there is always the hope that happiness is possible. As we later learn, these words fail to deter Welsh from committing suicide himself. The two say their goodbyes. Girleen seems to believe that they might stay in contact despite Welsh's departure, but as the scene closes it is obvious that Welsh believes they will not meet again.

Scene Five

Welsh sits centre stage, reciting the contents of his letter to Valene and Coleman. He criticises the pair for their actions: Coleman for murdering their father, and Valene for attempting to profit from that murder. Welsh believes that the brothers must once have loved each other, and urges them to recapture that love by forgiving the many things they have done to each other. He acknowledges that his faith in the pair might look foolish, but claims that he believes in their capacity to change.

Scene Six

We are back in the Connors' living-room. The shelves have been re-filled with religious figurines – this time, ceramic (and thus impossible to melt down). Coleman is again reading a women's magazine when Valene enters, carrying a plastic bag with yet more religious figurines. As in previous scenes, the pair argue about crisps and similarly trivial subjects, and again their inevitable recourse to violence is interrupted at a crucial moment by the arrival of someone from outside – in this case, Girleen, who has come to tell them that Father Welsh has committed suicide.

Girleen reveals that she has read Welsh's letter, and was appalled to learn that he was trusting that his death might induce Valene and Coleman to learn to love each other

again and thus redeem his soul from the eternal damnation
of a suicide. She had strong feelings for Welsh, she reveals,
and had been selling poteen only so that she could save
enough money to buy him a gift: a silver heart on a chain.
She flings the chain on the floor and runs from the house.

The two brothers are shocked by this revelation, and
agree that they will try to follow Welsh's request to be nice
to each other. The audience will suspect that the brothers'
attempt at reconciliation is unlikely to be successful,
however, as both callously laugh at the news that Welsh's
first name is Roderick.

Scene Seven

For the third time in the play, we begin the scene with
characters returning from a funeral – in this case, Father
Welsh's. Valene and Coleman have entered the room
together, and seem to be making an effort to be kind to each
other, sharing some vol-au-vents and a glass of poteen. In
general conversation, the two reveal that Girleen has
reacted badly to Welsh's death. They suggest that she is
likely to be committed to an institution for the mentally ill
before long.

The brothers begin to follow Welsh's instructions, taking
turns to confess something which the other brother must
then forgive. What should be an occasion for healing and
atonement quickly degenerates into yet another fight. The
two brothers become increasingly competitive, each trying
to make a revelation that is more outrageous and hurtful
than his brother's. Finally, Coleman confesses that he killed
Valene's dog, and provides the dog's ears as evidence. The
two brothers face off each other – Coleman holding a rifle
and Valene a knife, each threatening to kill the other.

Coleman has realised that Valene is so angry that the
threat of being shot is having no impact on him: he
therefore points the gun instead at the stove – which causes
Valene to stop immediately. Coleman shoots at the stove,
which explodes; he then smashes all of the religious figurines
to bits. The two brothers again confront each other, before

finally realising that they have failed miserably to follow Father Welsh's request and that he must therefore be 'burning in hell'. This realisation prompts yet another confession: that the brothers actually enjoy fighting with each other, because fighting shows that they really care about each other. Coleman finally admits that he didn't pay for Valene's house insurance (as Valene had suspected in Scene Two), which means that Valene will have to pay for a new stove. Coleman rushes out of the house, fleeing from his furious brother.

Devastated, Valene decides to burn Welsh's letter – but at the last moment he changes his mind and pins the letter to the crucifix, alongside Girleen's chain. Valene then leaves the house and, as the lights fade, the last thing the audience sees are the crucifix, the letter and the heart on the chain.

Commentary

Appearance and reality

Martin McDonagh first came to public attention in February 1996, when *The Beauty Queen of Leenane* was co-produced by London's Royal Court Theatre and Druid Theatre, a highly respected company based in the west of Ireland. The Druid director Garry Hynes had chosen the play as the first production for Galway's newly opened civic theatre, where it played for twelve performances. It was then brought on a three-venue tour of rural Ireland, before transferring to the Royal Court's sixty-seater Upstairs venue, where it ran for just under a month.

That first production was well received, by critics and audiences alike. But in those first few months of McDonagh's career, no one could have predicted that, within the next decade, he would become one of the world's most popular dramatists. By 2010, he had produced a further six plays, all of which had achieved success internationally – winning awards, being translated into dozens of languages and generating hundreds of critical and scholarly articles. He'd also become a respected film-maker, winning an Academy Award for his short film *Six Shooter* in 2006, and following up that success with the full-length hit *In Bruges*, which he wrote and directed.

Interestingly, he also became one of the world's most controversial dramatists during the same period. Scholars, critics and practitioners all began to question aspects of McDonagh's life and work, from his nationality to his originality. The strength of his popularity had provoked an equally strong backlash from the theatrical and academic establishment.

That curious mix of popular adulation and critical hostility was evident from an early stage in McDonagh's career. In 1997, he had achieved the unusual feat of having four of his plays running simultaneously in London's West End. *The Beauty Queen* had been joined by *A Skull in Connemara* and *The Lonesome West* to become *The Leenane Trilogy*; and, at the same time, the Royal National Theatre was staging *The Cripple of Inishmaan*, the first part of an *Aran Islands Trilogy*. The only other writer to have four plays appearing simultaneously in London that year was William Shakespeare. For a dramatist who had not been heard of eighteen months previously, McDonagh's achievement was unprecedented.

In Ireland, his plays were initially greeted with enthusiasm by audiences. Because of his mixture of dark humour and absurdism, McDonagh seemed to be working in the same tradition as John Millington Synge, Sean O'Casey, Brendan Behan, Samuel Beckett and many other great Irish dramatists – and he was praised for offering new perspectives on important Irish themes, such as emigration, familial relations, religion, gender and the land. McDonagh also seemed to point the way forward for Irish society at a time when the country was undergoing unprecedented change. On the one hand, it was experiencing new levels of liberalisation and prosperity: its unemployment rate had fallen to under 3 per cent, emigration was in decline, and prohibitive laws against homosexuality and divorce had been revoked. Yet on the other, many of the major authorities of Irish life were being severely undermined, due to revelations of political corruption, clerical child abuse and widespread institutional incompetence. McDonagh's first plays allowed Irish audiences to come to terms with these events. *The Beauty Queen of Leenane* exploded the myth of the happy Irish family only months after the legalisation of divorce. *A Skull in Connemara* suggested that Ireland was lawless and amoral, presenting an inept police officer at a time when the Irish police seemed to be losing their grip on organised crime. And *The Lonesome West* presented the Catholic Church in a state of dire crisis, at a time when the first revelations of clerical child abuse were emerging. So to those Irish audiences, McDonagh was an exciting new voice, whose work seemed powerful, urgent and liberating.

Yet even then, critics were uneasy about aspects of McDonagh's work. Many journalists and academics in Ireland began to express the fear that international audiences might think that McDonagh's version of Ireland was authentic: that he might be reinforcing negative stereotypes about the Irish as stupid, drunken, lazy, provincial, inarticulate and prone to acts of mindless violence. To an extent, those fears seemed justified when early British reviews of the plays appeared. For instance, Michael Billington of the *Guardian* told his readers that McDonagh's aim in *The Leenane Trilogy* was not to challenge Irish stereotypes, but to suggest that '*the reality* [about Ireland] is murder, self-slaughter, spite, ignorance and familial hatred'. Similarly, in 1999, one of the earliest regional US stagings of *The Beauty Queen* took place in Virginia, where the production's director declared outright that the play is 'a true representation of Ireland, particularly in the north'. Irish critics were horrified at the suggestion that international audiences might mistakenly see McDonagh's work as presenting the 'reality' or a 'true representation' of their country. But rather than criticise the people who had misunderstood McDonagh's plays, instead the critics attacked the writer himself.

Meanwhile, McDonagh was attracting negative commentary in Britain too, but for slightly different reasons. McDonagh, stated Penelope Dening in the *Irish Times*, has an 'undoubted ability to get up the nose of the theatrical establishment' in London. Aleks Sierz, for one, complained about McDonagh's comparison of himself to the young Orson Welles, and criticised his attack on older English playwrights for being 'so ugly' and 'really badly dressed' (*In-Yer-Face Theatre*, p. 205). Richard Eyre and Nicholas Wright relate the ensuing decline in McDonagh's popularity to the British public's concern that he was not as 'Irish' as they had initially thought. 'When McDonagh, in his many media appearances, turned out to be a chic young guy, wearing the nicest Armani suit you've ever seen and sporting a marked

South London accent, bemusement turned to fury,' they write. '"If this is an Irish playwright, I'm a banana," cried the chorus' (*Changing Stages*, p. 277). This comment is very revealing, since it appears to be based on the assumption that the terms 'chic young guy' and 'Irish playwright' are mutually exclusive – suggesting that McDonagh provoked criticism because he didn't match people's assumptions about what an Irish writer should be. Again, McDonagh was blamed when others misunderstood his work.

By 1999, both *The Beauty Queen* and *The Lonesome West* had made their way to Broadway, where both were successful. Yet in that same year, many English critics were declaring that McDonagh's career was effectively over. On his *In-Yer-Face Theatre* website, Aleks Sierz described McDonagh as an example of the 'writer as meteor: now you see him, now you don't'. His suggestion was that, having blazed brightly in 1997, McDonagh had since crashed inelegantly to earth. As Sierz himself acknowledges, rumours of McDonagh's demise were soon proved to be inaccurate, as first *The Lieutenant of Inishmore* (2001) and then *The Pillowman* (2003) premiered in the UK, in both cases to enormous acclaim. They were followed by the films *Six Shooter* (2005) and *In Bruges* (2008). And McDonagh's first American play, *A Behanding in Spokane*, opened in New York in March 2010, with Christopher Walken in the lead role. So the suggestion that McDonagh's career was over before it had really begun now seems ridiculous.

To a large extent, much of the initial negativity about McDonagh was provoked by comments made by (or attributed to) him in newspaper interviews. He first attracted the attention of the mainstream media when he was presented with the George Devine Award for Most Promising Newcomer in December 1996. At the Award Ceremony in London, McDonagh had a disagreement with the actor Sean Connery, and that incident was quickly picked up by the tabloid press – with the result that, in the words of Fintan O'Toole, McDonagh became famous overnight, not for his plays but for 'telling Sean Connery to fuck off'.

He soon found himself being widely presented as an iconoclastic figure who had little respect for theatrical tradition – the 'Johnny Rotten' of British drama. Theatre, McDonagh was quoted as saying, was the 'least interesting of the art forms'. He claimed to have learned how to write from watching Australian soap operas like *Neighbours* and *Home and Away*. We were told that he knew little or nothing about theatre – that he had never even read the plays of Synge, the Irish writer whose works seem to resemble his own so closely. And it was asserted that McDonagh was interested in writing only because he wanted 'to avoid having a real job'.

We now know that many of the media statements about McDonagh were exaggerated or presented out of context – and in some cases were inaccurate. If we think, for example, of Eyre and Wright's suggestion that McDonagh's popularity declined because British audiences were concerned about his not being 'Irish enough', it's worth noting that McDonagh never claimed to be either Irish or English. 'I always felt somewhere kind of in-between,' he told Fintan O'Toole in 1997:

> I'm happy having a foot in both camps. I'm not into any kind of definition, any kind of -ism, politically, socially, religiously, all that stuff. It's not that I don't think about those things, but I've come to a place where the ambiguities are more interesting than choosing a strict path and following it. (*Irish Times*, 26 April 1997)

And, far from being dismissive of other dramatists, McDonagh has often expressed his indebtedness to the American playwright David Mamet and the British writer Harold Pinter; he's also spoken of how his play *The Lieutenant of Inishmore* was influenced by the work of Joe Orton. And he has mentioned his admiration of the Argentinean writer Jorge Luis Borges: 'It's from him I began to appreciate the importance of telling a story,' said McDonagh in one of his first interviews (*Galway Advertiser*, 11 January 1996).

We also now know that, although McDonagh hadn't read Synge when he wrote his first plays, he was thoroughly familiar with that writer's work by the time his *Leenane Trilogy* was produced. 'I read *The Playboy of The Western World*', he told Fintan O'Toole in 1997, 'and the darkness of the story amazed me. I thought it would be one of those classics that you read in order to have read, rather than to enjoy, but it was great.' He also seemed to have been influenced by Samuel Beckett: his play *A Skull in Connemara* takes its title from a line in Beckett's *Waiting for Godot*, for example.

The reception of McDonagh's work was therefore determined by the fact that critics couldn't categorise him easily. His plays appeared to be Irish, but he himself was a 'chic' Londoner. They appeared to have been crafted with extraordinary care, yet McDonagh had stated that he'd written all of them during a few months in 1994 – and that *The Beauty Queen* had been completed in less than a week. They blurred the categories of high and low art, and narrowed the gap between the literary and the popular – reminding audiences of Beckett and Borges at one moment, and of the Sex Pistols and Tarantino at another. Perhaps, then, the best way to approach McDonagh's work is to look beyond such simplistic categories – we should, like McDonagh himself, seek to explore interesting ambiguities rather than follow strict paths. And we should also be aware of the difference between appearance and reality. That difference has dominated the creation of McDonagh's own public persona. And, as we'll see, it also plays a huge role in his plays.

Locating *The Lonesome West*

Because critics have occasionally claimed (inaccurately) that McDonagh has never read the plays of J.M. Synge, it's interesting to observe that *The Lonesome West* takes its title from Synge's 1907 Irish classic, *The Playboy of the Western World*.

In Synge's drama, a young man called Christy Mahon arrives at a pub in the west of Ireland, claiming to have

killed his father. That story so impresses the pub's owner –
the drunken and self-centred Michael James Flaherty – that
he instantly offers Christy a job. Christy will be employed as
the pub's 'pot-boy', and will therefore be able to protect
Flaherty's daughter Pegeen while the old man spends the
night getting drunk at a funeral. Pegeen's fiancé, the
effeminate and priest-fearing Shawn Keogh, had already
been asked to undertake this role, but had fled from the pub
when asked. His cowardice had provoked a disgusted
response from Flaherty. 'Oh, there's sainted glory this day
in the lonesome west,' he says to Pegeen, 'and by the will of
God I've got you a decent man!' (*Compete Plays 1*, London:
Eyre Methuen, 1981, p. 180). He's being entirely sarcastic
about his future son-in-law here: Shawn's 'saintliness' and
'decency' are regarded as negative rather than admirable
traits by Flaherty and his fellow villagers.

It's not surprising that McDonagh draws on this line for
his own play. For centuries, Ireland's western region has
been idealised as a place of stunning natural beauty, rich in
traditional culture and folklore. But Synge and McDonagh
both show that it's also a place that has been impoverished
in many ways – not just economically, but culturally and
(perhaps) intellectually also. The West is a wonderful place
to visit, they suggest; and it's a wonderful place to write
about too – but it doesn't seem to offer much to the people
who actually have to live there. In these plays, the
characters who are ambitious and talented can choose
between two options: to emigrate or, as happens more
frequently, to surrender to frustration and bitterness.
Everyone else gets on with the sad task of surviving from
one day to the next. It's little wonder, then, that Synge's and
McDonagh's most admirable characters feel so isolated,
despite being surrounded by countless other people. It is for
this reason that the word 'lonesome' and its variants appear
thirty-three times in Synge's play and nineteen times in
McDonagh's.

Also evident in that line from *The Playboy* is a dangerously
skewed sense of morality. The arrival in Flaherty's pub of a
man who has murdered his father should provoke a negative

response: fear, outrage, a desire to see justice done. Yet as Flaherty's sarcasm indicates, it is Christy's willingness to be violent, rather than Shawn's sense of morality, that is seen as a blessing – as a 'sainted glory' enacted through the 'will of God'. To Synge's original audiences in Ireland, this line seemed blasphemous. But what makes these words provocative even now is that they reveal a clash between the appearance and the reality of religious faith within Irish culture. The language of Synge's villagers is rich in religious allusion, yet it's also obvious that they have all failed completely to understand and internalise the central tenets of Christianity: forgiveness, compassion, charity, selflessness and, above all, love for others.

Synge's awareness of the difference between appearance and reality in Irish life is at the heart of *The Lonesome West*. McDonagh's uproarious tale about two warring brothers may owe much more to the films of the Marx Brothers than the biblical story of Cain and Abel, but behind the mayhem, serious questions are being asked. Is it possible to lead a genuinely good life? Does religion offer any solace from the hardship of everyday existence? Which is worse: to be completely isolated, or to be forced to live with someone you despise? And, given that the world seems full of hatred, despair and violence – why should we bother going on living? Such questions torment the characters in this play; they should also trouble the audience, who will find themselves laughing at truly terrible events. How, then, are these questions developed?

Violence, love and hate – Valene and Coleman

The plays of Martin McDonagh are dominated by stories about conflict between siblings. We might think of Helen and Bartley in *The Cripple of Inishmaan*, a brother and sister whose idea of playing together involves Bartley having eggs smashed over his head. Likewise, in *The Lieutenant of Inishmore*, a young woman called Mairead shows her feelings for her brother by shooting him repeatedly with an air rifle;

he in turn kidnaps her pet cat, inadvertently causing its death. A major feature of *A Skull in Connemara* is the relationship between Tom and Mairtin Hanlon, two brothers who appear to despise each other. Even in *The Beauty Queen of Leenane*, a poor relationship between siblings leads indirectly to disaster. That play's protagonist Maureen is forced to look after her elderly mother by herself: her sisters have long since abandoned the family home and make no effort to care for their mother – aside, that is, from sending a birthday wish to her on her favourite radio programme. And Maureen's would-be lover Pato fails to develop his relationship with her because he makes the mistake of trusting his brother to deliver a letter directly to her. Indeed, the only play by McDonagh that presents a positive relationship between siblings is *The Pillowman*. Turning morality upside-down, that play shows that the prosperity of its protagonist was founded on the misery of his brother – and it also shows that the greatest act of love one brother can perform for the other is to kill him. In this context, the relationship of Valene and Coleman Connor does not seem uniquely dysfunctional.

Perhaps the simplest explanation for the dominance of this theme in McDonagh's work is that stories about fraternal conflict are particularly dramatic. Many of the great plays of Shakespeare, for example, derive their energy from a conflict between brothers, as in *King Lear*, *As You Like It* and *Richard III*. That theme has also played an important role in many of the great twentieth-century dramas, such as Eugene O'Neill's *Long Day's Journey Into Night* (1955), Tom Murphy's *A Whistle in the Dark* (1961), Harold Pinter's *The Homecoming* (1965) and Sam Shepard's 1980 masterpiece, *True West*.

Indeed, it has often been suggested that McDonagh modelled *The Lonesome West* on *True West*. There is of course the obvious resemblance between the two titles, but the theme and structure of both plays are similar too. In McDonagh's play, two middle-aged brothers live in an isolated part of western Ireland; they fight endlessly with each other, but seem inseparable nevertheless. In Shepard's,

two middle-aged brothers called Lee and Austin are forced
to live together in their mother's house in the west coast of
the USA. As both stories unfold, the brothers move from ill-
humoured competitiveness with each other to outright
hostility – a mood that is worsened by their consumption of
large quantities of alcohol. In both plays, the conflict
between the pair is intensified by the intervention of a well-
meaning outsider (Father Welsh in McDonagh's play, a
Hollywood agent in Shepard's); and, in both plays, some of
the events are witnessed by a likeable but powerless woman
– Girleen in *The Lonesome West* and Mom in *True West*.
Kitchen appliances play an important role in both dramas,
with toasters appearing in Shepard's and a stove in
McDonagh's. And each writer explores – and perhaps seeks
to undermine – a national myth: the idea of the American
frontier west in *True West*, and the centrality of Catholicism
to Irish life in *The Lonesome West*.

It would be a little simplistic to call McDonagh's play an
Irish version of Shepard's, since *The Lonesome West* explores
many different ideas, reaches different conclusions, and has
a very different approach to language, characterisation and
humour. But there are certainly some interesting affinities
between the two plays. It should be noted in this context
that McDonagh told Sean O'Hagan in an interview in the
Guardian in 2001 that, of the twenty plays he'd seen before
he began writing himself, he'd only ever enjoyed three of
them. One was David Mamet's *American Buffalo*, another was
Tracy Letts's *Killer Joe* and the third was Shepard's *True
West*.

So it's certainly possible to think about *The Lonesome West*
in relation to great American drama. However, the
characterisation of Valene and Coleman can also be
considered in terms of a tradition within Irish theatre, in
which playwrights present pairs of men who are so
dysfunctional that they are forced to stay with each other in
order to survive – even though quite often they can barely
tolerate each other's company. This male double-act has a
strong presence throughout the history of Irish drama,
appearing in plays by Goldsmith, Wilde, O'Casey, Brian

Friel and many others.

Perhaps the most important dramatist to use this technique is Samuel Beckett. In his 1957 play *Endgame*, he presents us with a blind character called Hamm, who is dependent upon a servant-figure called Clov, whom he mistreats terribly. During the play, Hamm asks his companion why he stays with him and receives a blunt answer in response: 'because I don't have the combination to the larder' (*Complete Works*, London: Faber, 2006, p. 96). Hamm, that is, controls Clov's access to food, and therefore guarantees his subservience. This power struggle between two interdependent men in *Endgame* can fruitfully be compared to the relationship between Valene and Coleman. It's clear, for example, that one of the reasons Coleman continues to live with his brother is because he has nowhere else to go – a situation that Valene exploits mercilessly.

Perhaps the most famous example of the Irish male double-act is Vladimir and Estragon from another of Beckett's plays, *Waiting for Godot* (1955). Beckett's two tramps are utterly dependent on each other, yet they are also utterly bored with each other – and they appear to have concluded that the only thing worse than being together would be to separate. Valene and Coleman seem similar in many ways. They appear to hate each other, yet despite (or perhaps because of) their antipathy towards each other, they seem to find it impossible to live apart.

Yet as *The Lonesome West* moves towards its conclusion, audiences may find themselves wondering whether Valene and Coleman really hate each other as much as they claim. At the end of the play, the brothers will conclude that their fighting with each other 'does show you care' (p. 70) – they may be violent towards each other, but they are certainly not indifferent to one another. It is not clear whether either of the two brothers is capable of genuine love, however. They certainly don't appear to have been upset by the death of their father, who was killed by Coleman. That murder was provoked by the father making a relatively trivial comment about Coleman's hair. As Father Welsh points out, 'getting your hairstyle insulted is no just cause to go

murdering someone' (p. 45). Indeed, Coleman shows how
trivial his father's offence was when he himself insults
Maureen Folan's hairstyle, which, he claims, is like that of 'a
frightened red ape' (p. 61).

And, just as it was wrong for Coleman to shoot his father
over a throwaway remark, so too it was wrong for Valene to
seek to profit from that event. He agrees to tell the police
that their father's death was an accident, on the condition
that Coleman signs over his half of their father's estate to
Valene. 'Going lying that it was an accident just to get your
father's money is just as dark a deed as Coleman's deed, if
not more dark,' notes Father Welsh (p. 45). So given the
brothers' indifference to their father's death, it's difficult to
take entirely seriously their claim that they care about each
other.

Yet even if the brothers don't love each other, they do
seem to have a lot in common. They share a similar sense of
humour; they enjoy the same kinds of magazines and food;
and, while it would be absurd to describe them as having
values, they do have a similar moral outlook. It's also
apparent that the brothers despise their fellow villagers even
more than they hate each other. Coleman considers the
people who came to his father's funeral to be no more than
a 'pack of vultures', and he is scathingly critical of the seven
people who approached him to ask 'where the booze-up
after was to be held' – which is not a particularly
unreasonable question to ask about an Irish funeral (p. 6).
Valene, similarly, shows himself entirely unwilling to mourn
the death of Tom Hanlon later in the play, only able to
display what McDonagh terms 'phony empathy' (p. 27).

It's possible that the brothers' contempt for others arises
because they have failed to build a satisfying life for
themselves. Valene is undoubtedly a miser – he'd 'steal the
shite from a burning pig' according to Coleman (p. 6) – but
it's possible that he clings desperately to his belongings
because he has so little of value in the first place. It also
seems likely that he had tried to leave Leenane, judging
from the way he speaks in the play's third scene about
having spent time in England (p. 30). Although it's not made

explicit, this brief reference to the country implies that, like Mag in *Beauty Queen*, Valene had tried to make a better life for himself abroad, but was forced to return to Ireland.

Coleman also once had an opportunity for happiness. When he was at school, a girl called Alison O'Hoolihan had agreed to go on a date with him – but she had to go to hospital when the jealous Valene shoved her while she was chewing a pencil, and the date never happened. Coleman's pain seems heartfelt: 'I did fecking love Alison O'Hoolihan! We may've been married today if it hadn't been for that fecking pencil!' (p. 64). We might wonder why Coleman never sought out the company of any other woman. Valene offers one possible answer to that question, telling Coleman that 'Maureen Folan did once ask me to ask you if you wanted to see a film at the Claddagh Palace with her, and she'd've driven ye and paid for dinner too, and from the tone of her voice it sounded like you'd've been on a promise after, but I never passed the message onto ya, out of nothing but pure spite' (p. 61). In *Beauty Queen*, Maureen's chance of having a fulfilling relationship is destroyed when her mother fails to pass on a message from a would-be lover. We learn here that Valene has done the same thing to his own brother. Should we believe Valene's explanation that in destroying his brother's chance of a relationship, he was acting only out of spite? Or was he, like Maureen's mother Mag, simply terrified of being left alone?

Whatever the answer to that question, Father Welsh believes that the absence of women from Valene's and Coleman's lives is the main cause of their anger towards each other. 'Ye've lived in each other's pockets the entire of yere lives, and a sad and lonesome existence it has been, with no women to enter the picture for either of ye to calm ye down, or anyways not many women or the wrong sort of women,' he writes (pp. 45–6).

Welsh is probably correct in making this suggestion. We don't know what happened to the Connors' mother, who (significantly) is never mentioned in the play. And there's certainly plenty of evidence that the brothers are sexually frustrated. Coleman, for example, makes repeated reference to having things shoved up someone's 'arse' – from a vol-au-vent (p. 6), to a kettle (p. 17), to something unspecified that probably relates to crisps (p. 19). And both men seem obsessed with virginity. Coleman refers to his brother as a 'virgin fecking gayboy' three times (p. 23, 28, 49), while Valene uses that insult twice (p. 24, 27). Coleman also explains why Valene marks his property with the letter V. 'Do you think it's a 'V' for Valene?' he asks Father Welsh. 'It isn't. It's a V for Virgin, it is.' 'You're the king of the virgins,' retorts the enraged Valene (p. 25). Such insults reveal as much about the insecurities of the speaker as they do about the inadequacies of the victim. It seems likely that both men are unsure of themselves sexually, and that their homophobia and anger arise from confusion about their own sexuality.

The possibility that both men are indeed virgins is made most clear in the second scene, when Coleman pretends that he allowed Girleen to grope him in return for a free bottle of poteen. Valene finds this difficult to believe: 'Girleen wouldn't touch you below if you bought her a pony, let alone giving poteen away on top of it,' he states. Yet as Valene contemplates this possibility, it's clear that his own thoughts about sex are clouding his judgement. 'Eh?' he says, pausing. 'Girleen's pretty. (*Pause.*) Girleen's awful pretty. (*Pause.*) Why would Girleen be touching you below?' And then, pathetically, he asks a question that reveals his own inexperience: 'What did it feel like?' It's interesting that Coleman seems unable to invent a convincing lie in response, saying only that the 'touching below' was 'nice enough now' before distracting Valene's attention by stealing one of his packets of crisps (p. 21). Neither man is sexually experienced, yet each seems determined to prevent his brother from uncovering that truth.

Ninety years before *The Lonesome West* was written, Synge had written scathingly of the impact that forced celibacy was having on rural Irish life. 'If I was to tell all the sex-horrors I have seen [in the Irish countryside],' he wrote to a friend, 'I could a tale unfold that would wither up your blood' (Synge, *Collected Letters*, vol.1, Oxford: Clarendon Press, 1983, p. 76).

In his characterisation of Valene and Coleman, McDonagh
suggests that matters have not progressed much during the
intervening years. Valene and Coleman seem utterly
confused about sex and their sexual identify: the closest
either gets to understanding women, after all, lies in their
reading of magazines like *Woman's Own* and *Take a Break*.

The violence of Valene and Coleman probably arises
from that sexual frustration and the ensuing sense of
isolation. On the page, that violence seems harsh, but in
performance it will often seem cartoonish and largely
inconsequential. The pair grapple with each other on the
floor but never do any lasting damage; they may brandish
knives and point guns at each other, but they never seem
genuinely likely to kill each other. Nevertheless, some critics
have suggested that Valene and Coleman's relationship
could have deeper resonances, and that it acts as a
metaphor for civil conflict. Reading one of his women's
magazines, Valene mentions in passing 'a lad here in Bosnia
and not only has he no arms but his mammy's just died'
(p. 49). He doesn't seem to realise it, but he is reading an
article about a victim of the Yugoslav civil wars, which
raged from 1991 to 1995. It would be extravagant to suggest
that there is a link between the relationship of Valene and
Coleman on the one hand and the horrendous atrocities
that were committed in Bosnia on the other. Yet it can fairly
be said that, throughout *The Leenane Trilogy* and especially in
The Lonesome West, McDonagh is interested in understanding
how people who live in close proximity to each other (and
who should love each other) can end up hating each other
to such an extent that violence seems inevitable. This was an
important issue in the 1990s, a period that was dominated
by a series of bloody civil conflicts, not only in Bosnia but
also in Rwanda – and indeed in Northern Ireland too (as
we'll see later, some productions of *The Lonesome West* choose
to present the play as a metaphor for the Northern Irish
Troubles). *The Lonesome West* might therefore be compared
to plays that deal more explicitly with the theme of civil
conflict, such as Sarah Kane's *Blasted* (1995) and David
Edgar's *Pentecost* (1994). It's unlikely, however, that

McDonagh intended *The Lonesome West* to be taken only as a metaphor for a specific political conflict.

What separates *The Lonesome West* from plays like *Blasted* – and what marks it out as different from Sam Shepard's *True West* – is that McDonagh is not interested exclusively in the issue of violence. Rather, he uses that theme as the basis for a consideration of a much deeper issue: the way in which religion can be used to justify and obscure violence. In order to understand how and why this occurs, we need to consider the character of Father Welsh.

Redemption and suffering: Father Welsh

The figure of the priest dominates Irish drama – yet there is no one quite like Father Welsh in any other Irish play. There have certainly been negative portrayals of the clergy on the Irish stage before. Synge, for example, wrote a play called *The Tinker's Wedding*, which was first produced in 1909. It features a priest who agrees to marry a couple of 'tinkers', but only after they offer to pay him. That play concludes with the priest being tied up in a sack and held down by two of the female characters, who declare that it's 'little need we ever had for the like of you' (*Complete Plays*, p. 129). Other Irish plays have been more positive in their treatment of priests. One of the most popular Irish plays of the twentieth century was Frank Carney's *The Righteous Are Bold*. Premiering in 1946, Carney's play tells the story of an elderly priest who gives up his life to save a girl who's been possessed by a demon. It's largely forgotten now, but *The Righteous Are Bold* was hugely successful when it premiered, eventually transferring to Broadway. McDonagh's Father Welsh is rather unusual in Irish drama, because he comes somewhere between these two extremes: he lacks the authority and dignity of the priest in *The Righteous Are Bold*, but he is certainly not as ridiculous as the figure in *The Tinker's Wedding*. McDonagh clearly intends for us to sympathise with the character – but he does not want us to respect him unreservedly.

This blend of positive and negative traits in the characterisation of Welsh will be obvious to the audience from the play's first scene, when they are likely to form a negative impression of the priest owing to his obvious dependence on alcohol, even while they sympathise with him for having to endure Coleman's insults. Welsh claims that Leenane has driven him to drink: 'I never touched the stuff before I came to this parish,' he claims (p. 6). Leenane, as he points out, does seem like 'the murder capital of fecking Europe' (p. 38), and in any case he's not very highly respected by his parishioners. The first two plays in *The Leenane Trilogy* feature a running joke about how people can't even call Welsh by his correct name, referring to him as 'Father Welsh Walsh Welsh' – a joke repeated fourteen times in *The Lonesome West*.

So Welsh's life is difficult. Yet it seems likely that his fondness for alcohol arises from a desire to escape a deep-rooted sense of his own inadequacy. Actors and directors have adopted different approaches when attempting to convey this aspect of Welsh's personality. Some will portray him as a good person who's been corrupted by Leenane. Others will follow Coleman's line of thinking: Welsh may have been driven to drink, but 'some people don't need as much of a drive as others. Some need only a short walk' (p. 6). In such performances, actors seek to convey the notion that Welsh is simply making excuses, blaming Leenane for his own faults.

It's not clear whether Welsh drinks because he is a bad priest – or if he is a bad priest because he drinks. But there will be many times during *The Lonesome West* when those in the audience familiar with Catholicism will find themselves surprised by his apparent incompetence. Perhaps most seriously, Welsh violates one of the fundamental rules of his own Church when he breaks the seal of confession (that is, he reveals the sins that some of his parishioners have confessed). 'About betting on the horses and impure thoughts is all them bastards ever confess,' he says, with frustration. The embarrassed Coleman has to point out Welsh's error to him: 'Em, only I don't think you should be

telling me what people be confessing, Father. You can be
excommunicated for that I think' (p. 11). Welsh also reveals
that he is not very familiar with holy scripture. 'Thou
shouldst share and share alike the Bible says,' he suggests in
the play's third scene (p. 30). Although these words are
consistent with Christian teaching, they appear nowhere in
the Bible, or in any other religious texts. More importantly,
Welsh's interpretation of the Catholic Church's teachings
appears to be shaky, for instance when he says on p. 30,
'You can kill a dozen fellas, you can kill two dozen fellas. So
long as you're sorry after you can still get into heaven.'

Familiarity with rules and regulations and the ability to
quote scripture are not necessarily the only requirements
for being a good priest. Girleen clearly sees something
worth admiring in Welsh – not just as a man, but also in
his clerical role. Though her motives might be suspect, she
praises his sermon at the funeral of Tom Hanlon, for
instance: 'Almost made me go crying, them words did,' she
admits (p. 36). And Welsh also seems keen to see the best
in his parishioners – though it's not clear how we're
supposed to react to this feature of his personality. When
he learns of the suicide of Tom Hanlon, he describes him
as someone who 'never had a bad word to say about
anybody and did his best to be serving the community
every day of his life' (p. 26). Yet the audience – and
McDonagh's characters – know that this description is
inaccurate. Hanlon plays a major role in *Skull*, and is
shown there to be vindictive, malicious and in search of
self-advancement at all costs. Welsh, then, is either
hopelessly naive or is instead deliberately shutting his eyes
in describing Tom in this way.

It must also be pointed out, of course, that at the moment
when Tom committed suicide, Welsh was 'sitting pissed on
me own in a pub' (p. 29). '[Tom's] father had to haul me
drunk out of Rory's to say a prayer o'er him, and me
staggering,' says Welsh (p. 23). So his desire to speak well of
Tom could be seen as an attempt to compensate for his
inability to do something meaningful: to prevent the suicide
or console Tom's family adequately. Throughout *The*

Lonesome West, then, Welsh proves himself able to talk about what should be done, but rarely able to act for anyone's benefit, including his own.

The difference between Welsh's words and actions is probably most apparent in his decision to take his own life. As a Catholic, Welsh believes that a person who commits suicide will be condemned to hell. He hopes to escape that fate by restoring Coleman and Valene's love for each other: his suicide, therefore, is intended as a sacrifice that will shock the brothers into behaving well towards each other – a 'miracle' that will in turn save Welsh's soul.

This seems very noble: Welsh appears to imagine himself as being like one of the Christian martyrs whose statues Valene collects so enthusiastically. Yet it's probably worth asking whether he's being entirely sincere. After all, he regards himself as a 'shite' priest (p. 11), and seems to have nothing to live for. He is by his own admission 'maudlin' (p. 40); he's also obviously very lonely, and all of the characters mock him for his regular crises of faith (pp. 12, 14). In his suicide note (recited in Scene Five), Welsh suggest that the Connor brothers' anger with each other arises because they are 'lonesome' and because of the absence of women from their lives – but it's tempting to suggest that Welsh might be referring more to his own problems in this letter. Welsh believes that Tom Hanlon's suicide was inspired by courage, Guinness and stupidity – but isn't it possible that his own suicide arises from exactly the same causes? Despite his attempts to make his actions seem self-sacrificing, is Welsh just surrendering to his own sense of despair, using alcohol to fortify and religion to justify himself? McDonagh leaves this question for audiences to consider for themselves

Perhaps the most tragic aspect of Welsh's suicide is its impact on Girleen. Before his death, Welsh had said that Tom Hanlon took his own life because he had no one to tell him that his life was worth living. 'Where were his friends when he needed them in this decent world?' he asks. 'When he needed them most, to say, "Come away from there, ya daft, we'd miss ya, you're worthwhile, as dumb as you are."

Where were his friends then?' (p. 29). Welsh appears to
identify with Tom's isolation; indeed, it seems partially to
inspire his own thoughts of death. What Welsh doesn't
realise – through self-absorption or stupidity – is that he,
unlike Tom, has someone who believes that his life is worth
something. Girleen tells him that he certainly will be missed
when he leaves Leenane and asks him to keep in contact
with her. Welsh thanks her for her company – 'It's meant
something to me,' he says (p. 44) – but it doesn't stop him
from going through with his plan. Welsh's suicide, then, is
not just a rejection of his life; it's a rejection of the faith that
Girleen places in him.

So it makes sense that Girleen is so upset by the news of
Welsh's death – not just that he committed suicide, but that
he died in an attempt to redeem Valene and Coleman and
never even mentioned her in his letter. 'You notice he never
asked me to go saving his soul,' she says. 'I'd've liked to've
saved his soul. I'd've been honoured, but no . . . Only mad
drunken pig-shite feckbrained thicks he goes asking' (p. 53).
Of course, as a Catholic priest, Welsh is forbidden to marry
and has taken a vow of celibacy. Nevertheless, the real
tragedy for the character is that he lacks the awareness to
realise that redemption is available – not through his act of
self-sacrifice, but through Girleen's belief in him.

It is difficult, then, to determine precisely how we're
supposed to react to Welsh. Is he a bad priest but a good
Christian? Does he commit suicide from noble motives, or
is he simply trying to justify an act of gross selfishness? Does
he ignore Girleen's love for him because he is too self-
absorbed – or because he is so full of a sense of his own
failures that he has become blinded to the possibility that
someone else might care for him? Or is he aware of her
feelings but indifferent to them? And is he right to blame
Leenane for making him what he is? These are all difficult
questions to answer – but the impact of Leenane on its
inhabitants is worth exploring in a little more detail,
especially in relation to the characterisation of Girleen.

Words and actions: the characterisation of Girleen

McDonagh's plays are full of strong female characters, who are often far more assertive and powerful than their male counterparts. As mentioned, Helen in *The Cripple of Inishmaan* terrorises her brother Bartley and her employer the eggman – and she claims to have 'ruptured a curate' in the past. Likewise, Mairead in *The Lieutenant of Inishmore* shoots almost every other character in that play: 'you have some balls anyways,' she's told, with grudging admiration, by one of her eventual victims (p. 35). And of course Mag and Maureen from *Beauty Queen* are both formidable women in their own ways.

When we first encounter Girleen, she seems similar to such characters. We soon learn however that (yet again) there is a difference between appearance and reality – that Girleen's actions reveal far more than her words do. She seems at first to be an assertive and strong-willed individual. Despite being a schoolgirl, she shows in the first scene that she is perfectly willing to speak frankly about sexual matters to the three male characters. The local postman fancies her, she claims: 'I think he'd like to be getting into me knickers, in fact I'm sure of it' (p. 13). Later in that scene, she proves herself well able to stand up to Valene when he tries to underpay her for her poteen: 'You're the king of stink-scum fecking filth-bastards you, ya bitch-feck, Valene,' she tells him (p. 14).

However, Girleen is not as tough as she might at first have seemed. She sells poteen to the people in her community – which was against the law in Ireland when the play premiered. But she does so not because she is deliberately setting out to break the law, but rather because she wants to save enough money to buy Father Welsh a gift. And it seems likely that her sexual frankness arises not from experience, but from a desire to get the attention of Father Welsh, with whom she is clearly infatuated. This is made clear in the play's fourth scene, when a depressed Welsh states to Girleen that 'You have no morals at all, it seems', referring to her attitudes to sex and sexuality. Her response asserts her own value while implicitly rebuking Welsh: 'I have plenty of morals,' she says, 'only I don't keep whining on about them like some fellas' (p. 38).

The three male characters in *The Lonesome West* show an indifference to the value of life: Father Welsh commits suicide for reasons that are (to say the least) questionable, and Valene and Coleman appear to think nothing of the death of their father – or to worry much about the prospect of killing each other. Girleen, in contrast, sees the value of life. 'Even if you're sad or something, or lonely or something, you're still better off than them lost in the ground or in the lake, because . . . at least you've got the *chance* of being happy, and even if it's a real little chance, it's more than them dead ones have,' she states. 'At least when you're still here [alive] there's the *possibility* of happiness, and it's like them dead ones know that, and they're happy for you to have it. They say "Good luck to ya"' (pp. 42–43). Although expressed in simplistic language, this is an unusually eloquent passage, revealing Girleen's ability to do two things that the other characters are largely incapable of: she can empathise with other people's thoughts and feelings, and is able to define her life in relation to something positive – the possibility of happiness.

In many ways, then, Girleen is the most admirable character in the play. She talks like someone who is immoral and tough – yet she is much more vulnerable in reality. She can call Valene insulting names, and can tease a priest about condoms – but claims to be too shy to give a gift to Father Welsh: 'I'd've never've got up the courage to be giving it him to his face. I'd've blushed the heart out of me,' she admits, bitterly (p. 52). So in *The Lonesome West*, only Girleen seems capable of acting entirely on behalf of others, of loving others more than she loves herself. And it is interesting that she chooses to hide these aspects of her personality, pretending instead to be as immoral and rough as the other characters.

For that reason, audiences are likely to be upset by what happens to Girleen in the play's final scenes. Upon learning of Welsh's death, Girleen flings the heart and pendant she had bought for him to the floor of the Connors' living room. 'Feck me heart. Feck it to hell. Toss it into fecking skitter's the best place for that fecking heart,' she cries (p. 53). These words are probably intended to function both literally and metaphorically. Girleen's optimism – her belief in other people and her love for Welsh – have been betrayed: she has, to use the cliché, had her heart broken. She now claims to regret having wasted her money on Welsh. 'I should've skittered it away the boys in Carraroe, and not go pinning me hopes on a feck I knew full well I'd never have,' she says (p. 52). These words may sound like a dismissal of the priest, but alert audience members will know that Girleen is quoting almost exactly Welsh's earlier words to her (p. 39). By repeating these words about herself, Girleen reminds us that Welsh's opinion of her was much lower than it ought to have been. What is upsetting here is that she seems inclined to think that he might have been right.

As Welsh had suggested at the start of the play, Leenane seems like a place in which 'God has no jurisdiction' (p. 10). The barbaric behaviour of its under-twelves football team suggests that the next generation of Leenane people will be every bit as vicious as their elders. So the presence of Girleen might initially be seen as offering some hope that perhaps the future for Leenane is not quite as bleak as it might seem. Yet we learn at the end of the play that Father Welsh's suicide has had an appalling impact upon her. 'Her mam two times has had to drag her screaming from the lake at night . . . there where Father Walsh jumped, and her just standing there, staring,' Valene reports. 'It's the mental they'll be putting Girleen in before long if she carries on' (p. 58). It is a very grim ending for this character – the suggestion is that she too has finally been defeated by her environment. Watching these events unfold, audiences may form the conclusion that if Girleen has behaved better than the other characters during the play, this could be because she has not yet lived long enough to be worn down by Leenane.

Religion and the ethics of audience response

The characterisation of Girleen brings into focus a theme
that has been mentioned several times already: the
difference between appearance and reality, especially in
relation to religion. We've seen already that Father Welsh
might be using the rhetoric of religion to justify actions that
aren't especially virtuous, notably his suicide. Valene and
Coleman also seem to use religion to justify their actions.
'I'm sure to be getting into heaven,' says Valene, referring
not to the way that he lives his life, but instead to his
extensive collection of religious figurines (p. 47). Coleman
too is blithely confident of his salvation. 'Me, probably
straight to heaven I'll go, even though I blew the head off
poor Dad. So long as I go confessing to it anyways. That's
the good thing about being Catholic. You can shoot your
dad in the head and it doesn't even matter at all' (pp. 57–8).
The fault of both brothers here is to confuse a symbol with
the reality – to believe that the possession of religious
figurines is more important than genuine holiness, to believe
that an act of confession can result in absolution, even if it is
made without any genuine penitence.

   Central to this exploration of religion is a re-imagining of
two important features of the Catholic Church: confession
and a belief in the redemptive power of suffering. The
theme of confession and absolution runs through *The
Lonesome West* (indeed, it features in different ways in many
of McDonagh's works, especially *In Bruges*). We've seen
already that Coleman seems to understand the rules of
confession better than Father Welsh does, and there are
some very good jokes about that sacrament at the start of
the play. Yet in order to save his soul, Welsh encourages the
brothers to confess their sins not to him, or directly to God –
but to each other. 'Couldn't the both of ye, now, go
stepping back and be making a listeen of all the things about
the other that do get on yere nerves, and the wrongs the
other has done all down through the years that you still hold
against him, and be reading them lists out, and be discussing
them openly, and be taking a deep breath then and be

forgiving each other them wrongs, no matter what they may be?' Welsh asks. 'Would that be so awful hard, now?' (p. 46).

As we learn in the play's final scene, this act of confession and forgiveness is indeed 'awful hard' for the two brothers. Their competitive nature quickly overcomes their desire to abide by Father Welsh's request, and they attempt to outdo each other, each trying to make a revelation more outrageous and hurtful than the other. Just as the sacrament of confession is meaningless unless someone is genuinely repentant, so is Valene and Coleman's attempt to 'step back' and forgive each other revealed to be pointless, because neither brother really regrets his actions. McDonagh is not questioning the validity of the sacrament of confession here; rather, he is showing how that sacrament may be used by immoral people to convince themselves that their actions are without consequence.

A similar scrutiny is given to another of the central features of the Christian faith: the belief that Jesus suffered and died to redeem the sins of mankind. That belief has in turn given rise to the notion that certain forms of suffering can have a redemptive power. This focus on suffering is a feature of many religions, which place different levels of emphasis on activities like fasting or personal sacrifice – but it's a particularly strong feature of traditional Irish Catholicism. For example, not far from Leenane lies Croagh Patrick, a mountain that is strongly associated with Saint Patrick. Each year, thousands of pilgrims climb the mountain in honour of that saint – many doing so in their bare feet. The pain they inflict upon themselves is intended to be 'offered up': just as the pain of Christ can be considered positive when re-imagined in symbolic terms, so can the pain of the pilgrim be re-imagined as positive on a symbolic level. Likewise, all Catholics are encouraged during Lent (the forty-day period that leads up to Easter) to undertake some kind of personal sacrifice for the sake of spiritual enrichment.

Such activities are carried out for a variety of reasons, and are based on complex religious ideas – so it would be wrong to over-simplify them. Nevertheless, it is clear that one of the aims of *The Lonesome West* is to consider what happens when suffering is given a redemptive power (this theme also dominates *The Pillowman* and *In Bruges*). The idea is introduced to the audience in the play's third scene, when Welsh burns his hands in the molten plastic of Valene's saints. It seems at first that his act is grounded in despair at the news that Coleman deliberately murdered his father – and that Valene deliberately profited from that terrible event. '**Welsh** *stares at the two of them dumbstruck, horrified*,' writes McDonagh. '*He catches sight of the bowl of steaming plastic beside him and, almost blankly . . . clenches his fists and slowly lowers them into the burning liquid, holding them under*' (p. 35). These actions seem irrational, almost involuntary: Welsh carries them out 'almost blankly', we're told.

Yet he soon re-imagines that pain, giving it a symbolic importance. 'I have been thinking about ye non-stop since the night I did scald me hands,' he tells the brothers in his suicide note. 'Every time the pain does go through them hands I do think about ye, and let me tell you this. I would take that pain and pain a thousand times worse, and bear it with a smile, if only I could restore to ye the love for each other as brothers ye do so woefully lack' (p. 45). The pain that Welsh experiences encourages him to commit suicide: he believes that his pain – his death, in fact – can redeem Valene and Coleman. This, Welsh believes, would be 'the greatest achievement of his whole time' in Leenane (p. 46). So in addition to redeeming the brothers, Welsh is seeking to redeem himself.

But what does Welsh's suffering actually accomplish? By the end of the play, Valene and Coleman have few secrets from each other, but they seem largely unchanged from the way they were in the first scene. Girleen on the other hand has changed utterly, transformed from someone with a sense of hope to becoming almost ghost-like, haunting the place where Father Welsh committed suicide, and likely to be sent to a hospital for the mentally ill. If Welsh is a saintly martyr, just like one of Valene's plastic saints, McDonagh seems to be questioning seriously whether his sacrifice was worth it.

The link between suffering and redemption has long

dominated drama, from *King Oedipus* in ancient Greece to
King Lear in Jacobean London. So it is important to place
The Lonesome West in that broad historical context.
Nevertheless, it is also important to see McDonagh's
critique of Catholicism in the context of the time and place
where this play was premiered: Ireland in 1997. This was a
time when Irish society was just learning of the
institutionalised abuse, over many decades, of thousands of
the country's most vulnerable citizens by members of the
Catholic Church. Priests and nuns had systematically
abused children and young adults, both sexually and
physically – and, to make matters worse, church authorities
had actively facilitated that abuse, by moving guilty clergy
from one parish to another and by refusing to report their
actions to the police. For many members of McDonagh's
first Irish audiences, his jokes about Catholicism were
extraordinarily provocative. Seeking to reassure Father
Welsh, for instance, Coleman says 'you're a fine priest.
Number one you don't go abusing five-year-olds, so, sure,
doesn't that give you a head start over half the priests in
Ireland?' (p. 11) Later, Valene will describe Welsh as the
'laughing stock of the Catholic Church in Ireland',
vindictively adding that this 'takes some fecking doing, boy'
(p. 32). Those first Irish audiences were forced to think
about the fact that clerical abuse in that country lasted for
several decades, and that its impact is evident everywhere:
not just in the brothers' twisted sense of morality, but also in
their father's strange habit of screaming at nuns. This is not
to suggest that the focus on suffering within Catholicism
caused the physical and sexual abuse of children by priests.
Rather, there is an attempt here to reveal the extent to
which the public appearance of Catholicism in Ireland – the
use of religious statues, the public acts of faith – were
disguising acts of horrendous violence.

For the original Irish audience, then, the play's most
powerful moment – perhaps it's most transformative
moment too – occurs when Valene's religious figurines are
placed in the stove. McDonagh is literally showing us these
emblems of religion in meltdown, suggesting that these

public presentations of saintliness can be destroyed. It's at this moment that the clash between appearance and reality works most effectively: McDonagh shows that the appearance of religious power and authority (the statues) can disappear, in a literal puff of smoke.

Someone reading *The Lonesome West* for the first time could be forgiven for forming the view that the play is amoral. McDonagh presents us with an environment in which people who are good or admirable (like Girleen and Father Welsh) are doomed, whereas those who behave badly seem to be rewarded (such as the Connor brothers). It would be wrong, however, to believe that simply because McDonagh presents a particular vision of the world, he is saying that this is how things should be. Indeed, the power of *The Lonesome West* lies in the fact that it challenges its audiences to account for, react against and resolve the problems that it dramatises.

Perhaps the most significant moment in the play, then, is a discussion between Father Welsh and Girleen in the fourth scene. Welsh has realised that Maureen Folan killed her mother, and suspects strongly that Mick Dowd killed his wife (as explored in *A Skull in Connemara*). So the news that Coleman is also responsible for a murder has deeply affected him. But even more shocking to him is that Girleen was aware of these events long before he was – and that she did nothing. 'I think I did hear a rumour somewhere' about the murder, she concedes. 'A fecking rumour?' he replies. 'And you didn't bat an eye or go reporting it?' (p. 38)

This is a key moment in the play. Violence, abuse and brutality can arise from many causes, but Welsh shows his awareness that good people who do nothing to stop wrongdoing are themselves morally culpable. This suggestion resonated with the play's original Irish audience, reminding them that clerical child abuse was not simply a result of the Church's covering-up of its members' crimes – it was also enabled by a culture of silence that pervaded the entire society. Like Girleen, people in Ireland had for decades heard 'a rumour somewhere' about what was happening and (with some notable exceptions) had done nothing to prevent it. If McDonagh shows us that Irish Catholicism is in meltdown, he also challenges us to consider how the Church's power to enact atrocity was enabled by the silence of its own members.

Welsh's response helps us to understand the play's final moments. As the lights fade, a spotlight rests for a moment on three objects hanging on the wall centre stage: a crucifix, a letter from Father Welsh and a chain bought for him by Girleen. These three symbols mean nothing to Valene and Coleman. The crucifix signifies a kind of self-sacrifice that neither man can achieve, the letter is a call for a peace that neither man desires and the chain is a symbol of the love that neither man will ever experience. And all three are emblems of the suffering of innocent people. Why then does the light linger on this part of the set? Should the audience leave the theatre feeling hopeless, convinced that Valene and Coleman will never change? Perhaps.

But perhaps the purpose of those images is instead to force the audience to think about their own lives and their own responsibilities. *The Lonesome West* is of course primarily a comedy – and it presents us with characters and situations that exaggerate reality for comic effect. Nevertheless, the dilemmas at the heart of *The Lonesome West* are real enough. Like Synge before him, McDonagh is reminding us that *seeming* to be good and *being* good are rarely the same thing. We must, then, leave the theatre facing the question asked so poignantly by Father Welsh and Girleen. When we are confronted with intolerable brutality, what must we do in response? Will we sit quietly when confronted with knowledge – or will we do something to change matters?

Leenane – the murder capital of Europe?

One of the accusations most frequently levelled against McDonagh is that he is misrepresenting Ireland, making its inhabitants seem foolish and presenting Leenane as a place that has a depressing – perhaps even a corrupting – influence on its inhabitants. McDonagh's decision to set five of his produced plays in real Irish places undoubtedly contributes to this perception. But is it justified to say that McDonagh is attacking or exploiting Ireland?

To answer that question, it is probably worth observing that McDonagh has shown little interest in geographical authenticity in his two non-Irish plays. Shortly before the opening of *A Behanding in Spokane*, for instance, he explained to Gordon Cox that he'd never actually been to the American city that gives the play its title – though he did pass through it while asleep on a train. Why, then, did he name the play after Spokane? 'I always liked the word,' he explains. 'That K in the middle is really nice.' There's also a nice K-sound in the place-name for the setting of *The Pillowman*: Kamenice. We don't know which country that city is located in: a number of possibilities exist. As Werner Huber points out, 'Kamenice is a very common place-name in the Slavonic settlement areas of East Central Europe. Thus, we find, for example, ceská Kamenice (in Bohemia, Czech Republic), and also Saska Kamenice (in Saxony, where the German form is 'Chemnitz')' (*Literary Views on Post-War Europe*, p. 285). So all of McDonagh's locations can actually be found on a map, but that does not actually mean that the Kamenice or the Spokane referred to in the plays are intended to be understood as similar to the real places with those names.

This is also true of McDonagh's Irish locations. There are few resemblances between Leenane as it appears in *The Lonesome West* and the Leenane that actually exists in northern Galway. We are told that there is a church and graveyard in Leenane, but we are given no sense of their location in relation to the homes of the characters, or to other places in the village. Similarly, we are told that both Tom Hanlon and Father Welsh drown themselves in a lake, but the largest body of water in Leenane is actually Killary Harbour, a fjord – and a place of great natural beauty which dominates Leenane but is never mentioned in the *Trilogy*. We might also note that it is not the practice of the Irish police to station its members in the towns where they grew up, which makes it unlikely that Tom Hanlon in *Skull*

would be posted to Leenane (indeed, the real police station
in Leenane is staffed only two or three days a week by police
based in the nearby town of Clifden). So in short,
McDonagh's Leenane is an imagined location, bearing little
resemblance to the real Galway village.

Why, then, does McDonagh set his plays in that specific
locale? There are many possible explanations for this, but
perhaps the most intriguing is offered by Shaun Richards,
who suggests that the choice of Leenane allows McDonagh
to engage in 'close intertextual referencing'. What he means
by this is that 'characters and incidents seen in one play
become a topic of conversation in another' (*Irish University
Review*, 33, p. 204). It is not necessary to have seen *The Beauty
Queen* and *Skull* in order to appreciate *The Lonesome West*
fully, but as Richards points out, there are some intriguing
links between the three texts. Hence, our understanding of
The Lonesome West can be conditioned by our knowledge of
the other two plays.

If we watch or read the three plays in order, we're likely
to feel that they are becoming increasingly violent. In *The
Beauty Queen*, a daughter kills her mother with a poker, but
that event is shown off stage and occurs very late in the
action. In *Skull*, most of the violence again occurs off stage,
but there is a scene in which Mick Dowd and Mairtin
Hanlon smash several human skeletons to bits with mallets.
By the time we get to *The Lonesome West*, we may feel that
we've descended even further: in this play, much of the
violence *is* performed on stage, though it is often cartoonish
and rarely results in lasting damage. So our expectations of
what will happen in *The Lonesome West* are likely to be
conditioned by the violence presented in the previous two
plays. In *Beauty Queen*, the violence comes as a shock: we do
see Maureen torturing her mother, but we don't really
expect her to kill her. In *Skull*, we're never really sure if
Mick is guilty of having killed his wife. In both cases, then,
murder is something that will surprise and confuse the
audience. Yet in *The Lonesome West*, we're faced with a
reversal of that situation: Valene and Coleman seem
overwhelmingly likely to kill each other – but they don't

actually do so. Instead, the play's two deaths result from suicide. There are many ways of interpreting the development of the theme of violence across the three plays. We might see the reversal of the pattern in *The Lonesome West* as a typical example of McDonagh's ability to confound audience expectation. Yet it's also clear that *The Lonesome West* is intended to suggest that the situation in Leenane is gradually getting worse.

Also important is that a character in one play will often be referred to in another. These allusions are usually brief – and will probably go unnoticed by many – but they can deepen our understanding of the characters. For instance, Valene reveals that Maureen Folan once wanted to ask Coleman to go on a date with her. This revelation changes the way we think about both Connor brothers – but it will also change our understanding of Maureen, showing us that her desire to form a loving relationship in *Beauty Queen* had been thwarted at least once before. Furthermore, *Beauty Queen* makes occasional reference to the characters in *The Lonesome West*. In a letter to his family, Pato asks his brother to tell Girleen to stop falling in love with priests, for instance – showing that Leenane is a place where everyone knows everyone else's business, and that Girleen's feelings for Welsh had been obvious for a long time before the events described in *The Lonesome West*.

Beauty Queen and *Skull* also mention Father Welsh – who is always referred to as 'Father Welsh Walsh Welsh'. This means that audiences will be predisposed to find Welsh a little ridiculous even before he appears on stage: they've already been laughing at him during the previous two plays, after all.

This accumulation of information allows us to compare characters, themes and situations across the three plays. Each of the three plays features conflict between brothers: Ray and Pato in *Beauty Queen*, Tom and Mairtin in *Skull*, and Valene and Coleman in *The Lonesome West*. Superficially, the three relationships seem similar. Yet Mairtin's reaction to the suicide of his brother shows that even when two siblings appear to hold each other in contempt, they may still love each other. Audiences who have seen *A Skull in Connemara* are likely to be quite shocked by the way in which Tom and Mairtin are discussed in *The Lonesome West*. This will force them to reassess what they know about *Skull*, but it will also inevitably encourage them to believe that Welsh is right to think that Valene and Coleman might be able to find love for each other.

The purpose of the Leenane setting, then, is to give unity, credibility and depth to the three plays, by rooting them all in one shared location. It might be argued that McDonagh could have achieved this effect by setting the plays anywhere – and to an extent, that is true. But another benefit of using the setting of Leenane is that McDonagh can make use of the dialect of that region of Ireland.

Language

The language used by all of McDonagh's characters is a highly exaggerated version of 'Hiberno-English' (the technical term for English as it is spoken in Ireland). McDonagh explains how he came to develop the Irish 'voice' in his work. 'I wanted to develop some kind of dialogue style as strange and heightened as [Mamet's and Pinter's], but *twisted* in some way so the influence wasn't as obvious,' he told Fintan O'Toole. 'And then I sort of remembered the way my uncles spoke back in Galway, the structure of their sentences. I didn't think of it as structure, just as a kind of rhythm in the speech. And that seemed an interesting way to go, to try to do something with that language that wouldn't be English or American' (*Irish Times*, 26 April 1997). Like Synge before him – and as Mamet does with American English and Pinter with the English of London in such plays as *The Homecoming* – McDonagh takes elements of Hiberno-English and poeticises them.

He achieves this effect by paying particular attention to Hiberno-English vocabulary and grammar. For example, he uses many Irish slang words, such as 'feck', 'biteen', 'lube', 'skitter' and 'gob' during the play. He also reproduces the syntax of Hiberno-English, which involves organising sentences according to the rules of the Irish language, even though the words being used are English. For example, when Valene tells Welsh that 'a great parish it is you run' in the play's first scene (p. 10), he is breaking the rules of English syntax by placing the verb *you run* at the end of the sentence. In the Irish language, the verb would always appear in that place: Valene is therefore talking like someone who is thinking in Irish but speaking in English.

McDonagh also reproduces the verb tenses of Hiberno-English. The Irish language has a more complex version of the present tense than English does, and can therefore express a state called the 'habitual present', which can be used to describe the actions of a person who is doing something in the present moment that is part of a longer process. This construction appears constantly in the play, as for instance when Coleman tells Welsh that he can 'be doing what you like' or when Welsh in response says 'Don't be swearing today of all days' to Coleman (p. 5).

While Hiberno-English may add 'local colour' and humour to the script, it also enhances a technique that is used throughout the play – the use of rhythm, which works through repetition of sounds. If we consider the following example, we can see how repetition of the word 'check' has a rhythmic effect:

Valene   I'm checking.
Coleman   I can see you're checking.
Valene   I like to have a little check with you around.
Coleman   That's what you do best is check.
Valene   Just a biteen of a check, like. D'you know what I mean? In *my* opinion, like. (pp. 16–17)

The harshness of the word 'check' can seem almost violent when it is repeated so often; McDonagh's use of the Hiberno-English 'biteen' to interrupt this pattern helps to build tension, allowing the audiences to anticipate the carnage that is about to ensue.

It must be emphasised that, for McDonagh, this use of Irish speech arises for aesthetic reasons and not from a desire to be authentic. While all of the Hiberno-English used by McDonagh is derived from actual usage, no one in Ireland ever speaks like a character in a McDonagh play – any more than an Elizabethan Londoner would have spoken like a character in a Shakespeare play. So criticising McDonagh for his use of setting and language is rather to miss the point of his plays. As another McDonagh character puts it in *The Pillowman*, 'the only duty of a storyteller is to tell a story' – a line that could be seen as explaining McDonagh's own views on playwriting. McDonagh is motivated by a number of impulses in writing *The Leenane Trilogy*, but the desire to tell a good story has priority over most other considerations, including authenticity of setting and language.

Production history

The Lonesome West first appeared in 1997, when it was presented as part of *The Leenane Trilogy*, together with *The Beauty Queen of Leenane* and *A Skull in Connemara*. Co-produced by Druid Theatre and London's Royal Court Theatre, the *Trilogy* opened in Galway in June of that year, in a production that would tour both nationally and internationally until 2001. During those four years, the original productions of the *Trilogy* would be presented in thirty-one venues in Ireland (including the Aran Islands and Leenane itself). They were also produced, either individually or as the *Trilogy*, in England, Australia, the United States and Canada.

The Galway premiere of the *Trilogy* was well received, in part because audiences were given the opportunity to see all three plays in one day (as also occurred in London, Dublin and Sydney). This turned it into an 'event', and added to audiences' sense that they were seeing something exciting and unusual. The plays then transferred to London, where they were again very popular. After its West End run, the *Trilogy* played for a week in Cork, and then appeared for ten days at the 1997 Dublin Theatre Festival, where it was chosen as 'Reuters Play of the Year' by a three-person jury that included the playwright Marina Carr. Given that the Festival that year also featured new work from Robert Lepage and Thomas Kilroy, this was an impressive achievement.

McDonagh's international profile grew throughout 1998. The *Trilogy* appeared at the Sydney Festival, and *Beauty Queen* opened in New York, where it won four Tony Awards. *The Lonesome West* opened on Broadway in 1999 and, although it was less popular than *Beauty Queen*, it was nominated for four Tony Awards nevertheless. After its New York run, it returned to Ireland, enjoying a lengthy run at Dublin's Gaiety Theatre in 2001. The final performances of the Druid production were in Galway's Druid Lane Theatre in October 2001.

In order to understand the success of the original production of *The Lonesome West*, it is important to note the contribution of Garry Hynes, the artistic director of Druid Theatre. Widely regarded as Ireland's greatest living director, Hynes has had an important impact on the development of contemporary Irish playwriting by commissioning and directing some of the most significant plays of recent years, including Tom Murphy's *Bailegangaire* (1985) and Marina Carr's *Portia Coughlan* (1996). It was Garry Hynes who discovered McDonagh, finding his plays in the pile of unsolicited scripts that had been sent to Druid in 1994.

The reception of McDonagh's *The Leenane Trilogy* was also influenced by Hynes's directorial style. McDonagh is frequently described as a provocative playwright, but Hynes also has a history of challenging her audiences' assumptions, ideals and pieties, notably in her award-winning productions of work by Synge and Tom Murphy. As Fintan O'Toole observes, McDonagh's plays are an ideal vehicle for the acting style used by Hynes at Druid, which is famous for exploding 'naturalism from within, starting with the apparently familiar and making it very strange' (*Irish Times*). Hynes's style of direction for the *Trilogy* therefore was to present the absurd naturalistically. When she directed *The*

Lonesome West, she told Michael Ross that actors and director 'have to absolutely believe that Valene will not allow his brother to eat a packet of his Tayto [crisps]. If you think of that as a joke, and take that attitude to it in rehearsal, then the play doesn't exist' (*Sunday Times*, 18 May 2003). This presentation of the strange as if it were familiar was evident throughout Druid's production of the *Trilogy*, and accounts to a large extent for the plays' success.

Druid's rural and provincial tours of the *Trilogy* played an important role in developing McDonagh's reputation. A week before *Beauty Queen* transferred to the West End, it played in Leenane itself. Two months before *The Lonesome West* opened on Broadway, Druid cast Pat Shortt and Jon Kenny of the comedy duo D'Unbelievables in the play and brought them on an eleven-venue Irish tour. It is often suggested that McDonagh's work devalues rural Ireland, yet Druid's tours of his plays reveal the *value* of those places – asserting that a performance in Leenane can be just as important as a performance in New York, and that the reactions of audiences in the Aran Islands can be every bit as valid as those of the audiences in London.

In 1999, the rights were released to *The Leenane Trilogy*, after which some versions of the plays were produced independently of Druid and in ways that might be troubling for Irish audiences. Ian Kilroy notes that when Bernard Bloch directed and translated *The Lonesome West* as *L'Ouest Solitaire* at the 2002 Avignon Festival, he stated that 'the directorial approach will be to look at the fratricidal combat of the Connor brothers as a conflict reminiscent of the Northern conflict between Protestants and Catholics' (*Irish Times*, 6 July 2002). This suggestion that the senseless violence portrayed on stage might serve as a direct analogy for political violence in Northern Ireland seems simplistic, though, to be fair, audiences at Bloch's production did see the play in ways other than the narrowly political.

The Lonesome West has gone on to enjoy many productions on the international stage, in both professional and amateur settings. It is occasionally performed in repertory with Sam Shepard's *True West*, especially in the United States. It has also been performed many times in the UK, where it tends to be seen as a straightforward Irish comedy, in the spirit of the Channel 4 sitcom *Father Ted*. Within Ireland itself, it has been produced more often than any of McDonagh's other plays. In contrast to Bernard Bloch's suggestion that the play reveals the divisions in Northern Ireland, Belfast's Lyric Theatre and Donegal's An Grianán took *The Lonesome West* on a tour of Ireland in 2005. This made McDonagh's play one of the first to be co-produced by a theatre in Northern Ireland (the Lyric) and a theatre in the Republic of Ireland (An Grianán).

The play's continuing power over Irish audiences was revealed in 2009, when the Galway company Decadent Theatre revived *The Lonesome West* in a production directed by Andrew Flynn. His version of the play coincided with the release of two major reports into the abuse of children by members of the Catholic Church in Ireland. Whereas in 1997 many Irish members of McDonagh's audience were only starting to come to terms with these crimes, by 2009 revulsion against the acts of individual priests – and against the institution that covered up their crimes – was widespread. The presentation of Father Welsh in 2009 was therefore challenging in a new way: the Decadent production was asking us to sympathise with a priest at a time when the Catholic Church in Ireland was receiving widespread criticism and condemnation. This reveals the extent to which the play has – and will probably continue to have – a particular hold over audiences in Ireland.

Critical reaction

Academic critics have often been hostile towards McDonagh – both the man and his work. For many, he is exploiting anti-Irish stereotypes for financial gain, 'selling out' to the English, as Mary Luckhurst puts it. Victor Merriman suggests that McDonagh is to Irish drama what Jerry Springer is to American television: a showman who is exploiting 'white trash' for the amusement of a smug,

complacent and 'voyeuristic' middle-class audience
(*Cambridge Companion to Twentieth-Century Irish drama*, p. 254).
His defenders have argued that, in fact, McDonagh is
exploiting and undermining international audiences'
awareness of Irish stereotypes for dramatic as well as
political purposes.

However, the critical reception of McDonagh's work has
largely been determined by place: audiences tend to react to
his plays on the basis of their own local needs and interests.
The reception of McDonagh in London may, for example,
be considered in terms of his exposure of anxieties about
Ireland's role in British society in the 1990s. At the start of
that decade, Anglo-Irish relations were dominated by the
Troubles; by the turn of the century they were dominated
by the influx of Irish investment capital into British
commercial property. McDonagh's work plays
provocatively with the confusion generated by this
transformation. His plays are accused of presenting the
stereotypical Irish male as an inexplicably violent rural
caveman, feeding into stereotypes associated with the Irish
during the IRA's bombing campaign in England. Yet
McDonagh's own public persona plays against a new Irish
stereotype: the cosmopolitan *nouveau riche* Anglo-Irishman.
The *Trilogy* alludes constantly to the existence of anti-Irish
prejudice in Britain. McDonagh told Liz Hoggard in the
Independent that many aspects of Mag's description of her
time in London in *The Beauty Queen* 'came from stories my
mum told me – she worked in similar jobs when she first
came over from Ireland. And, like the play, she had to have
a black woman explain what those abusive words meant.'
It's interesting in this context to think again about the
comments of Eyre and Wright, who see McDonagh's 'Irish'
identity as problematic.

The plays reached Australia at a time when that country
was undergoing a growth in cultural self-confidence. Like
Ireland, Australia was becoming more aware of itself as
occupying a role on the global stage, and culture was an
important element in its attempt to come to terms with this
development. Hence, media coverage of *The Leenane Trilogy*

focused more on what the plays might be saying to Australia than on what they might be saying about Ireland. The Irish origin and setting of the plays were certainly considered, but considerably more attention was paid to McDonagh's thoughts about Australian soap opera. So while Irish critics worried about Australians taking McDonagh literally, in Australia his plays appear to have become part of that country's debate about how its own cultural exports influence overseas audiences.

Similarly, in New York, both *The Beauty Queen* and *The Lonesome West* were received in the context of American preoccupations. Whereas in Britain, McDonagh was presented as the 'bad boy' of British theatre, American journalists celebrated him as an example of the American 'rags to riches' narrative. A major news report broadcast on NBC focused on his overnight success, concluding with the message that 'McDonagh's take is five percent of the box office. So, with a good five-week run, he could leave America with $100,000 in his pocket' (the play, it should be noted, ran for almost a year). *The Lonesome West* was also viewed in relationships to American society. The play opened soon after 1999 high-school shootings in Colorado, in which a number of teenage students were killed – and so *The Lonesome West* became part of the debate about the relationship between violence and art in America, with Garry Hynes being called upon for her opinion on American gun-control in pre-publicity for the show (as reported by Philip Hopkin).

There is little evidence that audiences took *The Lonesome West* at 'face value' in America. In an interview with Diana Barth in *Irish Voice*, Maeliosa Stafford, who played Coleman in *The Lonesome West* on Broadway, stated that 'New York audiences "get" everything, they are with us, they understand Martin's dark humor.' Dawn Bradfield, who played Girleen in the same production, agreed, telling Michael Ross that she was surprised most by the conservatism of American audiences: 'there was a huge reaction to the bad language and to taking the piss out of the priest,' she said (*Sunday Times*, 23 November 2003).

The variety of critical reactions to McDonagh's plays suggests that his intention is not to convey one message that all of his audiences can understand and agree upon. Rather, he aims to force those audiences to undergo an experience unlike anything they know in their daily lives. They will find themselves experiencing a range of confusing emotions – laughing at the grotesque, terrified by the farcical, moved by the absurd. When confronted with such confusion, our only option is to look inwards, to ask what that confusion reveals about ourselves – our own morality, our own relationships, our own hopes and anxieties.

The Lonesome West may seem rooted to one place – a tiny village in the west of Ireland. And it may seem rooted to a very specific time – the early 1990s. Yet because of McDonagh's abilities to force us to look at ourselves, the play has a power that transcends the simple categories of time and place. *The Lonesome West* is about *us* – all of us – here and now: yesterday, today and tomorrow.

Further Reading

Plays and scripts by Martin McDonagh

Plays: 1, includes *The Beauty Queen of Leenane*, *A Skull in Connemara* and *The Lonesome West* (London: Methuen Drama, 1999)
The Cripple of Inishmaan (London: Methuen Drama, 1997)
The Pillowman (London: Faber, 2003)
In Bruges (London, Faber, 2008)
The Lieutenant of Inishmore, student edition (London: Methuen Drama, 2009)

Books and articles on McDonagh

Barth, Diana, 'Maeliosa's Malevolent Turn', *Irish Voice*, 11 May 1999

Billington, Michael, 'Excessive Talent for Plundering Irish Past', *Guardian*, 10 August 1997

Chambers, Lilian and Eamonn Jordan (eds), *A World of Savage Stories – The Theatre of Martin McDonagh* (Dublin: Carysfort Press, 2006)

Dening, Penelope, 'The Scribe of Kilburn', *Irish Times*, 18 April 2001

Eyre, Richard and Nicholas Wright, *Changing Stages: A View of British Theatre in the Twentieth Century* (London: Bloomsbury, 2000)

Hoggard, Liz, 'Playboy of the West End World', *Independent*, 15 June 2002

Hopkin, Philip, 'The Queen of Broadway is Back!', *Irish Voice*, 4 May 1999

Huber, Werner, 'From Leenane to Kamenice' in Christopher Housewitch (ed.), *Literary Views on Post-War Europe* (Trier: WVT, 2005), pp. 283–94

Luckhurst, Mary, 'Selling (-Out) to the English', *Contemporary*

Theatre Review, 14, 4, 2004, pp. 34–41

Mac Dubhghaill, Uinsionn, 'Drama Sails to Seven Islands', *Irish Times*, 27 November 1996

Merriman, Victor, 'Staging Contemporary Ireland: Heartsickness and Hopes Deferred' in Shaun Richards (ed.), *The Cambridge Companion to Twentieth-Century Irish Drama* (Cambridge University Press, 2004), pp. 244–257

NBC News Transcripts, 'Playwright Martin McDonagh Takes Broadway by Storm', *Today Show*, 16 April 1998

O'Hagan, Sean, 'The Wild West', *Guardian*, 24 March 2001

O'Toole, Fintan, 'Martin McDonagh is Famous for Telling Sean Connery to F*** Off. He Also Happens to be a Brilliant Playwright', *Guardian*, 2 December 1996

—, 'Nowhere Man', *Irish Times*, 26 April 1997

—, 'A Mind in Connemara: The Savage World of Martin McDonagh', *New Yorker*, 6 March 2006, pp. 40–7

Richards, Shaun, ' "The Outpouring of a Morbid, Unhealthy Mind": The Critical Condition of Synge and McDonagh', *Irish University Review*, 33, I, 2003, pp. 201–14

Ross, Michael, 'Hynes Means Business', *Sunday Times*, 18 May 2003

—, 'Dawn Bradfield is Rising Once Again as the Star of *Jane Eyre*', *Sunday Times*, 23 November 2003

Russell, Richard Rankin (ed.), *Martin McDonagh: A Casebook* (London: Routledge, 2007)

Books about Irish and British drama

Grene, Nicholas, *The Politics of Irish Drama* (Cambridge University Press, 1999)

Hynes, Jerome (ed.), *Druid: The First Ten Years* (Galway: Druid Performing Arts and the Galway Arts Festival, 1985)

Lonergan, Patrick, *Theatre and Globalization: Irish Drama in the Celtic Tiger Era* (Basingstoke and New York: Palgrave, 2009)

Morash, Christopher, *A History of Irish Theatre* (Cambridge University Press, 2001)

Pilkington, Lionel, *Theatre and Ireland* (Basingstoke: Palgrave, 2010)

Richards, Shaun, *The Cambridge Companion to Modern Irish Drama* (Cambridge University Press, 2004)

Roche, Anthony, *Contemporary Irish Drama* (Basingstoke: Palgrave, 2009)

Sierz, Aleks, *In-Yer-Face Theatre: British Drama Today* (London: Faber, 2001)

Websites

Sierz, Aleks, 'Martin McDonagh', www.inyerface-theatre.com

Druid Theatre, www.druid.ie (includes information about original productions of *The Leenane Trilogy*)

The Irish Playography, – www.irishplayography.com (production details of every Irish play produced since 1904)

A Hiberno-English Archive, http://www.hiberno-english.com

The Lonesome West

The Lonesome West, a Royal Court and Druid Theatre Company co-production, was first presented as part of 'The Leenane Trilogy' at the Town Hall Theatre, Galway, on 10 June 1997, and subsequently opened at the Royal Court Theatre Downstairs, St Martin's Lane, on 19 July 1997. The cast was as follows:

Girleen Kelleher   Dawn Bradfield
Father Welsh   David Ganly
Coleman Connor   Maelíosa Stafford
Valene Connor   Brían F. O'Byrne

Director Garry Hynes
Designer Francis O'Connor
Lighting Ben Ormerod
Sound Bell Helicopter
Music Paddy Cunneen

Characters

Girleen Kelleher
Father Welsh
Coleman Connor
Valene Connor

Setting

Leenane, a small town in Connemara, County Galway.

Scene One

The kitchen/living room of an old farmhouse in Leenane, Galway. Front door far right, table with two chairs down right, an old fireplace in the centre of the back wall, tattered armchairs to its right and left. Door to **Coleman**'s *room in the left back wall. Door to* **Valene**'s *room far left. A long row of dusty, plastic Catholic figurines, each marked with a black 'V', line a shelf on the back wall, above which hangs a double-barrelled shotgun and above that a large crucifix. A food cupboard on the wall left, a chest of drawers towards the right, upon which rests a framed photo of a black dog. As the play begins it is day.* **Coleman**, *dressed in black, having just attended a funeral, enters, undoing his tie. He takes a biscuit tin out of a cupboard, tears off the Sellotape that binds its lid and takes out from it a bottle of poteen, also marked with a 'V'.* **Father Welsh**, *a thirty-five-year-old priest, enters just behind him.*

Welsh   I'll leave the door for Valene.

Coleman   Be doing what you like.

He pours two glasses as **Welsh** *sits at the table.*

Coleman   You'll have a drink with me you will?

Welsh   I will, Coleman, so.

Coleman (*quietly*)   A dumb fecking question that was.

Welsh   Eh?

Coleman   I said a dumb fecking question that was.

Welsh   Why, now?

Coleman *gives* **Welsh** *his drink without answering and sits at the table also.*

Welsh   Don't be swearing today of all days anyway, Coleman.

Coleman   I'll be swearing if I want to be swearing.

Welsh   After us only burying your dad, I'm saying.

Coleman   Oh aye, right enough, sure you know best, oh aye.

Welsh (*pause*)   Not a bad turnout anyways.

Coleman   A pack of vultures only coming nosing.

Welsh   Come on now, Coleman. They came to pay their last respects.

Coleman   Did seven of them, so, not come up asking where the booze-up after was to be held, and Maryjohnny then 'Will ye be having vol-au-vents?' There'll be no vol-au-vents had in this house for the likes of them. Not while Valene holds the purse-strings anyways. If it was me held the purse-strings I'd say aye, come around for yourselves, even if ye are vultures, but I don't hold the purse-strings. Valene holds the purse-strings.

Welsh   Valene does be a biteen tight with his money.

Coleman   A biteen? He'd steal the shite out of a burning pig, and this is his poteen too, so if he comes in shouting the odds tell him you asked me outright for it. Say you sure enough demanded. That won't be hard to believe.

Welsh   Like an alcoholic you paint me as half the time.

Coleman   Well, that isn't a big job of painting. A bent child with no paint could paint you an alcoholic. There's no great effort needed in that.

Welsh   I never touched the stuff before I came to this parish. This parish would drive you to drink.

Coleman   I suppose it would, only some people don't need as much of a drive as others. Some need only a short walk.

Welsh   I'm no alcoholic, Coleman. I like a drink is all.

Coleman   Oh aye, and I believe you too. (*Pause.*) Vol-au-vents, feck. The white-haired oul ghoulish fecking whore. She's owed me the price of a pint since nineteen-seventy-fecking-seven. It's always tomorrow with that bitch. I don't care if she does have Alzheimer's. If I had a vol-au-vent I'd shove it up her arse.

Welsh   That's not a nice thing to be saying about a –

Coleman   I don't care if it is or it isn't.

Welsh (*pause*)   This house, isn't it going to be awful lonesome now with yere dad gone?

Coleman   No.

Welsh   Ah it'll be a biteen lonesome I'm sure.

Coleman   If you're saying it'll be a biteen lonesome maybe it *will* be a biteen lonesome. I'll believe it if you're forcing it down me throat and sure aren't you the world's authority on lonesome?

Welsh   Are there no lasses on the horizon for ye, now ye're free and easy? Oh I'll bet there's hundreds.

Coleman   Only your mammy.

Welsh   It's a beautiful mood today you're in. (*Pause.*) Were you never in love with a girl, so, Coleman?

Coleman   I was in love with a girl one time, aye, not that it's any of your fecking business. At tech this was. Alison O'Hoolihan. This gorgeous red hair on her. But she got a pencil stuck in the back of her gob one day. She was sucking it the pointy-end inwards. She must've gotten a nudge. That was the end of me and Alison O'Hoolihan.

Welsh   Did she die, Coleman?

Coleman   She didn't die, no. I wish she had, the bitch. No, she got engaged to the bastarding doctor who wrenched the pencil out for her. Anybody could've done that job. It didn't need a doctor. I have no luck.

Pause. **Welsh** *drinks some more.* **Valene** *enters with a carrier bag, out of which he takes some new figurines and arranges them on the shelf.* **Coleman** *watches.*

Valene   Fibreglass.

Coleman (*pause*)   Feck fibreglass.

Valene   No, feck you instead of feck fibreglass.

Coleman   No, feck you two times instead of feck fibreglass . . .

Welsh   Hey now!! (*Pause.*) Jesus!

Valene   He started it.

Welsh (*pause*)   Tom Hanlon I see he's back. I was speaking to him at the funeral. Did Tom know yere dad?

Coleman   Slightly he knew Dad. He arrested him five or six times for screaming at nuns.

Welsh   I remember hearing tell of that. That was an odd crime.

Coleman   Not that odd.

Welsh   Ah come on, now, it is.

Coleman   Oh if you say it is, Walsh, I suppose it is.

Valene   I do hate them fecking Hanlons.

Welsh   Why now, Val?

Valene   Why, is it? Didn't their Mairtin hack the ears off of poor Lassie, let him fecking bleed to death?

Coleman   You've no evidence at all it was Mairtin hacked the ears off of Lassie.

Valene   Didn't he go bragging about it to Blind Billy Pender?

Coleman   That's only hearsay evidence. You wouldn't get that evidence to stand up in a court of law. Not from a blind boy anyways.

Valene   I'd expect you to be agin me. Full well I'd expect it.

Coleman   That dog did nothing but bark anyways.

Valene   Well, barking doesn't deserve ears chopped off, Coleman. That's what dogs are supposed to do is bark, if you didn't know.

Coleman   Not at that rate of barking. They're meant to ease up now and then. That dog was going for the world's fecking barking record.

Welsh   And there's plenty enough hate in the world as it is, Valene Connor, without you adding to it over a dead dog.

Valene   Nobody'll notice a biteen more hate, so, if there's plenty enough hate in the world.

Welsh   A nice attitude that is for a −

Valene   Feck off and sling your sermons at Maureen Folan and Mick Dowd, so, if it's nice attitudes you're after, Walsh. Wouldn't that be more in your fecking line?

Welsh *bows his head and pours himself another drink.*

Coleman   That shut the fecker up.

Valene   It did. You see how quick he is to . . . That's my fecking poteen now! What's the . . . eh?

Coleman   He did come in pegging orders for a drink, now. What was I supposed to say to him, him just sticking Dad in the ground for us?

Valene   Your own you could've given him so.

Coleman   And wasn't I about to 'til I up and discovered me cupboard was bare.

Valene   Bare again, was it?

Coleman   Bare as a bald fella's arse.

Valene   Never unbare are your cupboards.

Coleman   I suppose they're not now, but isn't that life?

Welsh   And there's no such word as unbare.

Valene *stares at* **Welsh** *sternly.*

Coleman (*laughing*)   He's right!

Valene   Picking me up on me vocabulary is it, Welsh?

Coleman   It is, aye.

Welsh   I'm not now. I'm only codding ya, Val.

Valene   And shaking the hands of Mick and Maureen weren't you, too, I saw you at the grave there, and passing chit-chat among ye . . .

Welsh   I was passing no chit-chat . . .

Valene   A great parish it is you run, one of them murdered his missus, an axe through her head, the other her mammy, a poker took her brains out, and it's only chit-chatting it is you be with them? Oh aye.

Welsh   What can I do, sure, if the courts and the polis . . .

Valene   Courts and the polis me arse. I heard the fella you represent was of a higher authority than the courts and the fecking polis.

Welsh (*sadly*)   I heard the same thing, sure. I must've heard wrong. It seems like God has no jurisdiction in this town. No jurisdiction at all.

Valene *takes his bottle, mumbling, and pours himself a drink. Pause.*

Coleman   That's a great word, I think.

Valene   What word?

Coleman   Jurisdiction. I like J-words.

Valene   Jurisdiction's too Yankee-sounding for me. They never stop saying it on *Hill Street Blues.*

Coleman   It's better than unbare anyways.

Valene   Don't you be starting with me again, ya feck.

Coleman   I will do what I wish, Mr Figurine-man.

Valene   Leave me figurines out of it.

Coleman   How many more do ya fecking need?

Valene   Lots more! No, lots and lots more!

Coleman   Oh aye.

Valene   And where's me felt-tip pen, too, so I'll be giving them me 'V'?

Coleman   I don't know where your fecking felt-tip pen is.

Valene   Well, you had it doing beards in me *Woman's Own* yesterday!

Coleman Aye, and you wrenched it from me near tore me hand off.

Valene Is all you deserved . . .

Coleman You probably went hiding it then.

On these words, **Valene** *instantly remembers where his pen is and exits to his room. Pause.*

Coleman He's forever hiding things that fella.

Welsh I'm a terrible priest, so I am. I can never be defending God when people go saying things agin him, and, sure, isn't that the main qualification for being a priest?

Coleman Ah there be a lot worse priests than you, Father, I'm sure. The only thing with you is you're a bit too weedy and you're a terror for the drink and you have doubts about Catholicism. Apart from that you're a fine priest. Number one you don't go abusing five-year-olds, so, sure, doesn't that give you a head start over half the priests in Ireland?

Welsh That's no comfort at all, and them figures are over-exaggerated anyways. I'm a terrible priest, and I run a terrible parish, and that's the end of the matter. Two murderers I have on me books, and I can't get either of the beggars to confess to it. About betting on the horses and impure thoughts is all them bastards ever confess.

Coleman Em, only I don't think you should be telling me what people be confessing, Father. You can be excommunicated for that I think. I saw it in a film with Montgomery Clift.

Welsh Do ya see? I'm shite sure.

Coleman Too hard on yourself is all you are, and it's only pure gossip that Mick and Maureen murdered anybody, and nothing but gossip. Mick's missus was a pure drink-driving accident is unfortunate but could've happened to anybody . . .

Welsh With the scythe hanging out of her forehead, now, Coleman?

Coleman   A pure drink-driving, and Maureen's mam only fell down a big hill and Maureen's mam was never steady on her feet.

Welsh   And was even less steady with the brains pouring out of her, a poker swipe.

Coleman   She had a bad hip and everybody knew, and if it's at anybody you should be pegging murder accusations, isn't it me? Shot me dad's head off him, point-blank range.

Welsh   Aye, but an accident that was, and you had a witness . . .

Coleman   Is what I'm saying. And if Valene hadn't happened to be there to see me tripping and the gun falling, wouldn't the town be saying I put the barrel bang up agin him, blew the head off him on purpose? It's only because poor Mick and Maureen had no witnesses is why all them gobshites do go gossiping about them.

Valene *returns with his pen and starts drawing 'V's on the new figurines.*

Welsh   See? You do see the good in people, Coleman. That's what I'm supposed to do, but I don't. I'm always at the head of the queue to be pegging the first stone.

Valene   He's not having another fecking crisis of faith?

Coleman   He is.

Valene   He never stops, this fella.

Welsh   Aye, because I have nothing to offer me parish at all.

Coleman   Sure haven't you just coached the under-twelves football to the Connaught semi-finals yere first year trying?

Welsh   Ah the under-twelves football isn't enough to restore your faith in the priesthood, Coleman, and we're a bunch of foulers anyway.

Coleman   Ye aren't. Ye're skilful.

Welsh   Ten red cards in four games, Coleman. That's a world's record in girls' football. That'd be a record in boys' football. One of the lasses from St Angela's she's still in hospital after meeting us.

Coleman   If she wasn't up for the job she shouldn't've been on the field of play.

Welsh   Them poor lasses used to go off crying. Oh a great coach I am, oh aye.

Coleman   Sissy whining bitches is all them little feckers are.

A rap on the front door, then **Girleen**, *a pretty girl of seventeen, puts her head round it.*

Girleen   Are ye in need?

Valene   Come in for yourself, Girleen. I'll be taking a couple of bottles off ya, aye. I'll get me money.

He exits to his room as **Girleen** *enters, taking two bottles of poteen out of her bag.*

Girleen   Coleman. Father Welsh Walsh Welsh . . .

Welsh   Welsh.

Girleen   Welsh. I know. Don't be picking me up. How is all?

Coleman   We've just stuck our dad in the ground.

Girleen   Grand, grand. I met the postman on the road with a letter for Valene.

She lays an official-looking envelope on table.

That postman fancies me, d'you know? I think he'd like to be getting into me knickers, in fact I'm sure of it.

Coleman   Him and the rest of Galway, Girleen.

Welsh *puts his head in his hands at this talk.*

Girleen   Galway minimum. The EC more like. Well, a fella won't be getting into my knickers on a postman's wages. I'll tell you that, now.

Coleman   Are you charging for entry so, Girleen?

Girleen   I'm tinkering with the idea, Coleman. Why, are you interested? It'll take more than a pint and a bag of Taytos, mind.

Coleman   I have a three-pound postal order somewhere I never used.

Girleen   That's nearer the mark, now. (*To* **Welsh**.) What kind of wages do priests be on, Father?

Welsh   Will you stop now?! Will you stop?! Isn't it enough for a girl going round flogging poteen, not to go talking of whoring herself on top of it?!

Girleen   Ah, we're only codding you, Father.

She fluffs her fingers through **Welsh***'s hair. He brushes her off.*

Girleen (*to* **Coleman**)   He's not having another crisis of faith is he? That's twelve this week. We should report him to Jesus.

Welsh *moans into his hands.* **Girleen** *giggles slightly.* **Valene** *enters and pays* **Girleen**.

Valene   Two bottles, Girleen.

Girleen   Two bottles it is. You've a letter there.

Coleman   Buy me a bottle, Valene. I'll owe ya.

Valene (*opening letter*)   Buy you a bottle me arse.

Coleman   Do ya see this fella?

Girleen   You've diddled me out of a pound, Valene.

Valene *pays up as if expecting it.*

Valene   It was worth a go.

Girleen   You're the king of stink-scum fecking filth-bastards you, ya bitch-feck, Valene.

Welsh   Don't be swearing like that now, Girleen . . .

Girleen   Ah me hairy arse, Father.

Valene (*re letter*)   Yes! It's here! It's here! Me cheque! And look how much too!

Valene *holds the cheque up in front of* **Coleman**'s *face.*

Coleman   I see how much.

Valene   Do ya see?

Coleman   I see now, and out of me face take it.

Valene (*holding it closer*)   Do ya see how much, now?

Coleman   I see now.

Valene   And all to me. Is it a closer look you do need?

Coleman   Out of me face take that thing now.

Valene   But maybe it's closer you need to be looking now . . .

Valene *rubs the cheque in* **Coleman**'s *face.* **Coleman** *jumps up and grabs* **Valene** *by the neck.* **Valene** *grabs him in the same way.* **Girleen** *laughs as they struggle together.* **Welsh** *darts drunkenly across and breaks the two apart.*

Welsh   Be stopping, now! What's the matter with ye?

Welsh *gets accidentally kicked as the brothers part. He winces.*

Coleman   I'm sorry, Father. I was aiming at that feck.

Welsh   Hurt that did! Bang on me fecking shin.

Girleen   You'll know now how the lasses at St Angela's be feeling.

Welsh   What's the matter with ye at all, sure?

Valene   He started it.

Welsh   Two brothers laying into each other the same day their father was buried! I've never heard the like.

Girleen   It's all because you're such a terrible priest to them, Father.

Welsh *glares at her. She looks away, smiling.*

Girleen   I'm only codding you, Father.

Welsh   What kind of a town is this at all? Brothers fighting and lasses peddling booze and two fecking murderers on the loose?

Girleen   And me pregnant on top of it. (*Pause.*) I'm not really.

Welsh *looks at her and them sadly, moving somewhat drunkenly to the door.*

Welsh   Don't be fighting any more, now, ye's two. (*Exits.*)

Girleen   Father Walsh Welsh has no sense of humour. I'll walk him the road home for himself, and see he doesn't get hit be a cow like the last time.

Coleman   See you so, Girleen.

Valene   See you so, Girleen. (**Girleen** *exits. Pause.*) That fella, eh?

Coleman (*in agreement*)   Eh? That fella.

Valene   Jeez. Eh? If he found out you blew the head off Dad on purpose, he'd probably get three times as maudlin.

Coleman   He takes things too much to heart does that fella.

Valene   Way too much to heart.

Blackout.

Scene Two

Evening. Against the back wall and blocking out the fireplace is now situated a large, new, orange stove with a big 'V' scrawled on its front. **Coleman**, *in glasses, sits in the armchair left, reading* Woman's Own, *a glass of poteen beside him.* **Valene** *enters, carrying a bag. Slowly, deliberately, he places a hand on the stove in a number of places in case it's been used recently.* **Coleman** *snorts in disgust at him.*

Valene   I'm checking.

Coleman   I can see you're checking.

Valene   I like to have a little check with you around.

Coleman   That's what you do best is check.

Valene   Just a biteen of a check, like. D'you know what I mean? In *my* opinion, like.

Coleman   I wouldn't touch your stove if you shoved a kettle up me arse.

Valene   Is right, my stove.

Coleman   If you fecking paid me I wouldn't touch your stove.

Valene   Well, I won't be fecking paying you to touch me stove.

Coleman   I know well you won't, you tight-fisted feck.

Valene   And *my* stove is right. Did *you* pay the three hundred? Did *you* get the gas fixed up? No. Who did? Me. My money. Was it your money? No, it was my money.

Coleman   I know well it was your money.

Valene   If you'd made a contribution I'd've said go ahead and use me stove, but you didn't, so I won't.

Coleman   We don't even need a stove.

Valene   You may not need a stove, but I need a stove.

Coleman   You never fecking eat, sure!

Valene   I'll start! Aye, by Christ I'll start. (*Pause.*) This stove is mine, them figurines are mine, this gun, them chairs, that table's mine. What else? This floor, them cupboards, everything in this fecking house is mine, and you don't go touching, boy. Not without me express permission.

Coleman   It'll be hard not to touch your fecking floor, now.

Valene   Not without me express . . .

Coleman   Unless I go fecking levitating.

Valene   Not without me express . . .

Coleman   Like them darkies.

Valene (*angrily*)   Not without me express fecking permission I'm saying!

Coleman   Your express permission, oh aye.

Valene   To *me* all this was left. To me and me alone.

Coleman   'Twasn't left but 'twas *awarded*.

Valene   Me and me alone.

Coleman   Awarded it was.

Valene   And you don't go touching. (*Pause.*) What darkies?

Coleman   Eh?

Valene   What darkies go levitating?

Coleman   Them darkies. On them carpets. Them levitating darkies.

Valene   Them's Pakis. Not darkies at all!

Coleman   The same differ!

Valene   Not at all the same differ! Them's Paki-men, same as whistle at the snakes.

Coleman   It seems like you're the expert on Paki-men!

Valene   I *am* the expert on Paki-men!

Coleman   You probably go falling in love with Paki-men too, so! Oh I'm sure.

Valene   Leave falling in love out of it.

Coleman   What did you get shopping, Mister 'I-want-to-marry-a-Paki-man'?

Valene   What did I get shopping, is it?

He takes two figurines out of his bag and arranges them delicately on the shelf.

Coleman   Ah for feck's sake . . .

Valene Don't be cursing now. Coleman. Not in front of the saints. Against God that is.

He takes eight packets of Taytos out of the bag and lays them on the table.

And some Taytos I got.

Coleman Be getting McCoys if you're getting crisps.

Valene I'll be getting what I li—

Coleman Ya fecking cheapskate.

Valene (*pause. Glaring*) I'm not getting some crisps taste exactly the same, cost double, Coleman.

Coleman They don't taste the same and they have grooves.

Valene They do taste the same and feck grooves.

Coleman Taytos are dried fecking filth and everybody knows they are.

Valene The crisp expert now I'm listening to. What matter if they're dried fecking filth? They're seventeen pee, and whose crisps are they anyways? They're my crisps.

Coleman They're your crisps.

Valene My crisps and my crisps alone.

Coleman Or get Ripples.

Valene Ripples me arse and I don't see you digging in your . . . what's this?

*He picks up **Coleman**'s glass and sniffs it.*

Coleman What's wha?

Valene This.

Coleman Me own.

Valene Your own your arse. You've no money to be getting your own.

Coleman I do have.

Valene   From where?

Coleman   Am I being interrogated now?

Valene   You are.

Coleman   Feck ya so.

Valene *takes his poteen out of his biscuit tin to check if any is missing.*
Coleman *puts the magazine aside, takes his glasses off and sits at the table.*

Valene   You've been at this.

Coleman   I haven't at all been at that.

Valene   It seems very . . . reduced.

Coleman   Reduced me arse. I wouldn't be at yours if you shoved a fecking . . .

Valene (*sipping it, uncertain*)   You've topped it up with water.

Coleman   Be believing what you wish. I never touched your poteen.

Valene   Where would you get money for . . . Me house insurance?! Oh you fecker . . . !

He desperately finds and examines his insurance book.

Coleman   I paid in your house insurance.

Valene   This isn't Duffy's signature.

Coleman   It is Duffy's signature. Doesn't it say 'Duffy'?

Valene   You paid it?

Coleman   Aye.

Valene   Why?

Coleman   Oh to do you a favour, after all the favours you've done me over the years. Oh aye.

Valene   It's easy enough to check.

Coleman   It *is* easy enough to check, and check ahead, ya feck. Check until you're blue in the face.

Confused, **Valene** *puts the book away.*

Coleman   It's not only money can buy you booze. No. Sex appeal it is too.

Valene   Sex appeal? You? Your sex appeal wouldn't buy the phlegm off a dead frog.

Coleman   You have your own opinion and you're well entitled to it. Girleen's of the opposite opinion.

Valene   Girleen? Me arse.

Coleman   Is true.

Valene   Eh?

Coleman   I said let me have a bottle on tick and I'll be giving you a big kiss, now. She said, 'If you let me be touching you below, sure you can have a bottle for nothing.' The deal was struck then and there.

Valene   Girleen wouldn't touch you below if you bought her a pony, let alone giving poteen away on top of it.

Coleman   I can only be telling the God's honest truth, and how else would I be getting poteen for free?

Valene (*unsure*)   Me arse. (*Pause.*) Eh? (*Pause.*) Girleen's pretty. (*Pause.*) Girleen's awful pretty. (*Pause.*) Why would Girleen be touching you below?

Coleman   Mature men it is Girleen likes.

Valene   I don't believe you at all.

Coleman   Don't so.

Valene (*pause*)   What did it feel like?

Coleman   What did what feel like?

Valene   The touching below.

Coleman   Em, nice enough now.

Valene (*unsure*)   I don't believe you at all. (*Pause.*) No, I don't believe you at all.

Coleman *opens and starts eating a packet of* **Valene***'s crisps.*

Valene   Girleen wouldn't be touching you below. Never in the world would Girleen be touching y— (*Stunned.*) Who said you could go eating me crisps?!

Coleman   Nobody said.

Valene   In front of me?!

Coleman   I decided of me own accord.

Valene   You'll be paying me seventeen pee of your own accord so! And right now you'll be paying me!

Coleman   Right now, is it?

Valene   It is!

Coleman   The money you have stashed?

Valene   And if you don't pay up it's a batter I'll be giving you.

Coleman   A batter from you? I'd be as scared of a batter from a lemon.

Valene   Seventeen pee I'm saying!

Pause. **Coleman** *slowly takes a coin out of his pocket and, without looking at it, slams it down on the table.*

Valene (*looks at the coin*)   That's ten.

Coleman *looks at the coin, takes out another one and slams that down also.*

Coleman   You can keep the change.

Valene   I can keep the change, can I?

He pockets the coins, takes out three pee, opens one of **Coleman**'s *hands and places the money in it.*

Valene   I'm in no need of charity.

He turns away. Still sitting, **Coleman** *throws the coins hard at the back of* **Valene**'s *head.*

Valene   Ya fecker ya!! Come on so!

Coleman *jumps up, knocking his chair over.*

Coleman   Come on so, is it?

Valene   Pegging good money at me?!

Coleman   It is. And be picking that money up now, for your oul piggy-bank, ya little virgin fecking gayboy ya . . .

The two grapple, fall to the floor and roll around scuffling. **Welsh** *enters through the front door, slightly drunk.*

Welsh   Hey ye's two! Ye's two! (*Pause. Loudly.*) Ye's two!

Coleman (*irritated*)   Wha?

Welsh   Tom Hanlon's just killed himself.

Valene   Eh?

Welsh   Tom Hanlon's just killed himself.

Valene (*pause*)   Let go o' me neck, you.

Coleman   Let go o' me arm so.

The two slowly let go of each other and stand up, as **Welsh** *sits at the table, stunned.*

Welsh   He walked out into the lake from the oul jetty there. Aye, and kept walking. His body's on the shingle. His father had to haul me drunk out of Rory's to say a prayer o'er him, and me staggering.

Valene   Tom Hanlon? Jeez. Sure I was only talking to Tom a day ago there. The funeral.

Welsh   A child seen him. Seen him sitting on the bench on the jetty, a pint with him, looking out across the lake to the mountains there. And when his pint was done he got up and started walking, the clothes still on him, and didn't stop walking. No. 'Til the poor head of him was under. And even then he didn't stop.

Coleman (*pause*)   Ah I never liked that Tom fecking Hanlon. He was always full of himself, same as all fecking coppers . . .

Welsh (*angrily*)   The poor man's not even cold yet, Coleman Connor. Do you have to be talking that way about him?

Coleman   I do, or if I'm not to be a hypocrite anyways I do.

Valene   It's hypocrites now. Do you see this fella, Father? Ate a bag of me crisps just now without a by your leave . . .

Coleman   I paid you for them crisps . . .

Valene   Then says he's not a hypocrite.

Coleman   I paid thruppence over the odds for them crisps, and how does eating crisps make you a hypocrite anyways?

Valene   It just does. And interfering with a schoolgirl on top of it is another crime, Father.

Coleman   I interfered with no schoolgirl. I was interfered with *be* a schoolgirl.

Valene   The same differ!

Welsh   What schoolgirl's this, now?

Coleman   Girleen this schoolgirl is. This afternoon there she came up and a fine oul time we had, oh aye.

Welsh   Girleen? Sure Girleen's been helping me wash the strips for the under-twelves football all day, never left me sight.

Embarrassed, **Coleman** *gets up and moves towards his room.* **Valene** *blocks his way.*

Valene   Aha! Aha! Now who's the virgin fecking gayboy, eh? Now who's the virgin fecking gayboy?

Coleman   Out of me way, now.

Valene   *Now*, eh?

Coleman   Out of me way I'm saying.

Valene   I knew well!

Coleman   Are you moving or am I moving ya?

Valene   *Now* did I know well? Eh?

Coleman   Eh?

Valene   Eh?

Welsh   Coleman, come back now. We –

Coleman   And you can shut your fecking gob too, Welsh or Walsh or whatever your fecking name is, ya priest! You don't go catching Coleman Connor out on lies and expect to be . . . and be expecting to . . . to be . . .

He enters his room, slamming its door.

Valene   You're a stuttering oul ass, so you are! 'To be . . . to be . . . to be . . . ' (*To* **Welsh**.) Eh?

As **Valene** *turns back to* **Welsh**, **Coleman** *dashes out, kicks the stove and dashes back to his room,* **Valene** *trying and failing to catch him.*

Valene   Ya fecker, ya!

He checks the stove for damage.

Me good fecking stove! If there's any damage done to this stove it'll be you'll be paying for it, ya feck! Did you see that, Father? Isn't that man mad? (*Pause.*) Do ya like me new stove, Father? Isn't it a good one?

Coleman (*off*)   Do ya see that 'V' on his stove, Father? Do you think it's a V for Valene? It isn't. It's a V for Virgin, it is.

Valene   Oh is it now . . . ?

Coleman (*off*)   V for Virgin it is, uh-huh.

Valene   When you're the king of the virgins?

Coleman (*off*)   Valene the Virgin that V stands for.

Valene   The fecking king of them you are! And don't be listening at doors!

Coleman (*off*)   I'll be doing what I wish.

Valene *checks stove again.* **Welsh** *is on the verge of tears.*

Valene (*re stove*)   No, I think it's okay, now . . .

Welsh You see, I come in to ye . . . and ye're fighting. Fair enough, now, that's all ye two ever do is fight. Ye'll never be changed. It's enough times I've tried . . .

Valene Are you crying, Father, or is it a bit of a cold you do have? Ah it's a cold . . .

Welsh It's crying I am.

Valene Well, I've never seen the like.

Welsh Cos I come in, and I tell ya a fella's just gone and killed himself, a fella ye went to school with . . . a fella ye grew up with . . . a fella never had a bad word to say about anybody and did his best to be serving the community every day of his life . . . and I tell you he's killed himself be drowning, is a horrible way to die, and not only do ye not bat an eye . . . not only do ye not bat an eye but ye go arguing about crisps and stoves then!

Valene I batted an eye.

Welsh I didn't notice that eye batted!

Valene I batted a big eye.

Welsh Well, I didn't notice it, now!

Valene (*pause*) But isn't it a nice stove, Father?

Welsh *puts his head in his hands.*

Valene *goes to the stove.*

Valene Only a day I've had it fixed up. You can still smell as clean as it is. Coleman's forbid to touch it at all because Coleman didn't contribute a penny towards it, for Coleman doesn't *have* a penny to contribute towards it. (*Picks up the three pee.*) He has three pee, but three pee won't go too far towards a stove. Not too far at all. He threw this three pee at me head earlier, d'you know? (*In realisation, angrily.*) And if he has no money and he wasn't interfered with, where the feck was it that poteen did come from?! Coleman . . . !

Welsh (*screamed*) Valene, you fecking fecker ya!!

Valene Wha? Oh, aye, poor Thomas.

He nods in phoney empathy.

Welsh (*pause. Sadly, standing*)   I came up to get ye to come to the lake with me, to be dragging poor Tom's body home for himself. Will ye be helping now?

Valene   I will be, Father. I will be.

Welsh (*pause*)   Feck. Two murders and a suicide now. Two murders and a fecking suicide . . .

He exits, shaking his head.

Valene (*calling out*)   Sure, not your fault was it, Father. Don't you be getting maudlin again! (*Pause.*) Coleman? I'm off down –

Coleman (*off*)   I heard.

Valene   Are ya coming so?

Coleman (*off*)   Not at all am I coming. To go humping a dead policeman about the country? A dead policeman used to laugh at me press-ups in PE? I don't fecking think so, now.

Valene   You forever bear a grudge, you. Ah anyways it's good strong men Father Walsh does need helping him, not virgin fecking gayboys couldn't pay a drunk monkey to go interfering with him.

He quickly exits. **Coleman** *storms into the room to find him gone. He goes to the door and idles there, thinking, looking around the room. His gaze falls on the stove. He picks up some matches and opens the stove door.*

Coleman   A virgin fecking gayboy, is it? Shall we be having gas mark ten for no reason at all, now? We shall, d'you know?

He lights the stove, turns it up, closes its door and exits to his room. He returns a few seconds later and looks around the room.

For no reason at all, is it?

He takes a large oven-proof bowl out of a cupboard, places all of the figurines from the shelf into the bowl and puts the bowl inside the stove, closing its door afterwards.

Now we'll be seeing who's a virgin gayboy couldn't pay a
monkey to interfere with him. I'll say we'll fecking see.

*He pulls on his jacket, brushes his unkempt hair for two seconds with
a manky comb, and exits through the front door. Blackout.*

Scene Three

A few hours later. **Valene** *and* **Welsh** *enter, slightly drunk.* **Valene**
takes his poteen out of his tin and pours himself a glass. **Welsh** *eyes it
a little.*

Valene   That was an awful business, eh?

Welsh   Terrible. Just terrible, now. And I couldn't say a thing
to them. Not a thing.

Valene   What could be said to them, sure? The only thing
they wanted to hear was 'Your son isn't dead at all', and that
wouldn't have worked. Not with him lying in their front room,
dripping.

Welsh   Did you ever hear such crying, Valene?

Valene   You could've filled a lake with the tears that family
cried. Or a russaway at minimum.

Welsh (*pause*)   A wha?

Valene   A russaway. One of them russaways.

Welsh   Reservoir?

Valene   Russaway, aye, and their Mairtin crying with the
best of them. I've never seen Mairtin crying as hard. I suppose
that's all you deserve for chopping the ears off a poor dog.

Welsh   I suppose if it's your only brother you lose you do cry
hard.

Valene   I wouldn't cry hard if I lost me only brother. I'd buy
a big cake and have a crowd round.

Welsh   Ah Valene, now. If it's your own brother you can't get on with, how can we ever hope for peace in the world . . . ?

Valene   Peace me arse and don't keep going on, you. You always do whine on this oul subject when you're drunk.

He sits at the table with drink and bottle.

Welsh (*pause*)   A lonesome oul lake that is for a fella to go killing himself in. It makes me sad just to think of it. To think of poor Tom sitting alone there, alone with his thoughts, the cold lake in front of him, and him weighing up what's best, a life full of the loneliness that took him there but a life full of good points too. Every life has good points, even if it's only . . . seeing rivers, or going travelling, or watching football on the telly . . .

Valene (*nodding*)   Football, aye . . .

Welsh   Or the hopes of being loved. And Thomas weighing all that up on the one hand, then weighing up a death in cold water on the other, and choosing the water. And first it strikes you as dumb, and a waste, 'You were thirty-eight years old, you had health and friends, there was plenty worse-off fecks than you in the world, Tom Hanlon' . . .

Valene   The girl born with no lips in Norway.

Welsh   I didn't hear about her.

Valene   There was this girl in Norway, and she was born with no lips at all.

Welsh   Uh-huh. But then you say if the world's such a decent place worth staying in, where were his friends when he needed them in this decent world? When he needed them most, to say, 'Come away from there, ya daft, we'd miss ya, you're worthwhile, as dumb as you are.' Where were his friends then? Where was I then? Sitting pissed on me own in a pub. (*Pause.*) Rotting in hell now, Tom Hanlon is. According to the Catholic Church anyways he is, the same as every suicide. No remorse. No mercy on him.

Valene   Is that right now? Every suicide you're saying?

Welsh   According to us mob it's right anyways.

Valene   Well, I didn't know that. That's a turn-up for the books. (*Pause.*) So the fella from *Alias Smith and Jones*, he'd be in hell?

Welsh   I don't know the fella from *Alias Smith and Jones*.

Valene   Not the blond one, now, the other one.

Welsh   I don't know the fella.

Valene   He killed himself, and at the height of his fame.

Welsh   Well, if he killed himself, aye, he'll be in hell too. (*Pause.*) It's great it is. You can kill a dozen fellas, you can kill two dozen fellas. So long as you're sorry after you can still get into heaven. But if it's yourself you go murdering, no. Straight to hell.

Valene   That sounds awful harsh. (*Pause.*) So Tom'll be in hell now, he will? Jeez. (*Pause.*) I wonder if he's met the fella from *Alias Smith and Jones* yet? Ah, that fella must be old be now. Tom probably wouldn't even recognise him. That's if he saw *Alias Smith and Jones* at all. I only saw it in England. It mightn't've been on telly here at all.

Welsh (*sighing*)   You wouldn't be sparing a drop of that poteen would ya, Valene? I've an awful thirst . . .

Valene   Ah, Father, I have only a drop left and I need that for meself . . .

Welsh   You've half the bottle, sure . . .

Valene   And if I had some I'd spare it, but I don't, and should priests be going drinking anyways? No they shouldn't, or anyways not on the night . . .

Welsh   Thou shouldst share and share alike the Bible says. Or somewhere it says . . .

Valene   Not on the night you let one of your poor flock go murdering himself you shouldn't, is what me sentence was going to be.

Welsh   Well, was that a nice thing to be saying?! Do I need that, now?!

Valene (*mumbling*)   Don't go trying to go cadging a poor fella's drink off him so, the wages you're on.

He gets up, puts the bottle back in his biscuit tin and carefully Sellotapes the lid up, humming as he does so.

Welsh   Is there a funny smell off of your house tonight, Val, now?

Valene   If you're going criticising the smell of me house you can be off now, so you can.

Welsh   Like of plastic, now?

Valene   Cadging me booze and then saying me house smells. That's the best yet, that is.

Welsh (*pause*)   At least Coleman came down to help us with poor Thomas after all, even if he was late. But that was awful wrong of him to go asking Tom's poor mam if she'd be doing vol-au-vents after.

Valene   That was awful near the mark.

Welsh   And her sitting there crying, and him nudging her then, and again and again, 'Will ye be having vol-au-vents, Missus, will ye?'

Valene   If he was drunk you could excuse it, but he wasn't. It was just out of spite. (*Laughing.*) Although it was funny, now.

Welsh   Where is he anyways? I thought he was walking the road with us.

Valene   He'd stopped to do up his shoelaces a way back. (*Pause. In realisation.*) Coleman *has* no shoelaces. He has only loafers. (*Pause.*) Where have all me Virgin Marys gone?!

He leans in over the stove, placing his hands on its top, to see if the figurines have fallen down the back. The searing heat from the stove burns his hands and he pulls them away, yelping.

(*Hysterical.*) Wha?! Wha?!

Welsh   What is it, Valene? Did you go leaving your stove on?

Stunned, **Valene** *opens the stove door with a towel. Smoke billows out. He takes the steaming bowl of molten plastic out, sickened, places it on the table and delicately picks up one of the half-melted figurines with the towel.*

Welsh   All your figurines are melted, Valene.

Valene (*staggering backwards*)   I'll kill the feck! I'll kill the feck!

Welsh   I'll be betting it was Coleman, Valene.

Valene   That's all there is to it! I'll kill the feck!

Valene *pulls the shotgun off the wall and marches around the room in a daze, as* **Welsh** *jumps up and tries to calm him.*

Welsh   Oh Valene now! Put that gun down!

Valene   I'll blow the head off him! The fecking head off him I'll blow! I tell him not to touch me stove and I tell him not to touch me figurines and what does he do? He cooks me figurines in me stove! (*Looking into bowl.*) That one was blessed be the Pope! That one was given me mammy be Yanks! And they're all gone! All of them! They're all just the fecking heads and bobbing around!

Welsh   You can't go shooting your brother o'er inanimate objects, Valene! Give me that gun, now.

Valene   Inanimate objects? Me figurines of the saints? And you call yoursel' a priest? No wonder you're the laughing stock of the Catholic Church in Ireland. And that takes some fecking doing, boy.

Welsh   Give it me now, I'm saying. Your own flesh and blood this is you're talking of murdering.

Valene   Me own flesh and blood is right, and why not? If he's allowed to murder his own flesh and blood and get away with it, why shouldn't I be?

Welsh   What are you talking about, now? Coleman shooting your dad was a pure accident and you know well.

Valene   A pure accident me arse! You're the only fecker in Leenane believes that shooting was an accident. Didn't Dad make a jibe about Coleman's hairstyle, and didn't Coleman dash out, pull him back be the hair and blow the poor skulleen out his head, the same as he'd been promising to do since the age of eight and Da trod on his Scalectrix, broke it in two . . .

Coleman *enters through the front door.*

Coleman   Well, I did love that Scalectrix. It had glow-in-the-dark headlamps.

Valene *turns and points the gun at* **Coleman**. **Welsh** *backs off moaning, hands to his head.* **Coleman** *nonchalantly idles to the table and sits down.*

Welsh   It can't be true! It can't be true!

Coleman   Look at that fella gone pure white . . .

Valene   No, shut up, you! Don't be coming in mouthing after your fecking crimes . . .

Welsh   Tell me you didn't shoot your dad on purpose, Coleman. Please, now . . .

Valene   This isn't about our fecking dad! This is about me fecking figurines!

Coleman   Do you see this fella's priorities?

Valene   Melting figurines is against God outright!

Welsh   So is shooting your dad in the head, sure!

Valene   And on gas mark ten!

Welsh   Tell me, Coleman, tell me, please. Tell me you didn't shoot your dad there on purpose. Oh tell me, now . . .

Coleman   Will you calm down, you? (*Pause.*) Of course I shot me dad on purpose.

Welsh *starts groaning again.*

Coleman   I don't take criticising from nobody. 'Me hair's like a drunken child's.' I'd only just combed me hair and there was nothing wrong with it! And I know well shooting your dad in the head is against God, but there's some insults that can never be excused.

Valene   And cooking figurines is against God on top of it, if they're Virgin Mary figurines anyways.

Coleman   Is true enough, be the fella with the gun, and I'll tell you another thing that's against God, before this fella puts a bullet in me . . . (*To* **Welsh**.) Hey, moany, are you listening . . . ?

Welsh   I'm listening, I'm listening, I'm listening . . .

Coleman   I'll tell you another thing that's against God. Sitting your brother in a chair, with his dad's brains dripping down him, and promising to tell everyone it was nothing but an accident . . .

Valene   Shut up now, ya feck . . .

Coleman   So long as there and then you sign over everything your dad went and left you in his will . . .

Welsh   No . . . no . . . no . . .

Coleman   His house and his land and his tables and his chairs and his bit of money to go frittering away on shitey-arsed ovens you only got to torment me, ya feck . . .

Welsh   No, now . . . no . . .

Valene   Be saying goodbye to the world, you, fecker!

Coleman   And fecking Taytos then, the worst crisps in the world . . .

Valene *cocks the gun that's up against* **Coleman**'s *head.*

Welsh   No, Valene, no!

Valene   I said say goodbye to the world, ya feck.

Coleman   Goodbye to the world, ya feck.

Valene *pulls the trigger. There is a hollow click. He pulls the trigger again. Another click. A third time, and another click, as* **Coleman** *reaches in his pocket and takes out two shotgun cartridges.*

Coleman   Do you think I'm fecking stupid, now? (*To* **Welsh**.) Did you see that, Father? My own brother going shooting me in the head.

Valene   Give me them fecking bullets, now.

Coleman   No.

Valene   Give me them bullets I'm saying.

Coleman   I won't.

Valene   Give me them fecking . . .

Valene *tries to wrench the bullets out of* **Coleman**'s *clenched fist,* **Coleman** *laughing as he does so.* **Valene** *grabs* **Coleman** *by the neck and they fall to the floor, grappling, rolling around the place.* **Welsh** *stares at the two of them dumbstruck, horrified. He catches sight of the bowl of steaming plastic beside him and, almost blankly, as the grappling continues, clenches his fists and slowly lowers them into the burning liquid, holding them under. Through clenched teeth and without breathing,* **Welsh** *manages to withhold his screaming for about ten or fifteen seconds until, still holding his fists under, he lets rip with a horrifying high-pitched wail lasting about ten seconds, during which* **Valene** *and* **Coleman** *stop fighting, stand, and try to help him . . .*

Valene   Father Walsh, now . . .

Coleman   Father Walsh, Father Walsh . . .

Welsh *pulls his fists out of the bowl, red raw, stifles his screams again, looks over the shocked* **Valene** *and* **Coleman** *in despair and torment, smashes the bowl off the table and dashes out through the front door, his fists clutched to his chest in pain.*

Welsh (*exiting, screaming*)   Me name's *Welsh*!!!

Valene *and* **Coleman** *stare after him a moment or two.*

Coleman   Sure that fella's pure mad.

Valene   He's outright mad.

Coleman   He's a lube. (*Gesturing at bowl.*) Will he be expecting us to clear his mess up?

Valene *puts his head out the front door and calls out.*

Valene   Will you be expecting us to clear your mess up, you?

Coleman (*pause*)   What did he say?

Valene   He was gone.

Coleman   A lube and nothing but a lube. (*Pause.*) Ah it's your fecking floor. You clean it up.

Valene   You wha?!

Coleman   Do you see me nice bullets, Valene?

Coleman *rattles his two bullets in* **Valene**'s *face, then exits to his room.*

Valene   Ya fecking . . . !

Coleman's *door slams shut.* **Valene** *grimaces, pauses, scratches his balls blankly and sniffs his fingers. Pause. Blackout.*

Interval.

Scene Four

A plain bench on a lakeside jetty at night, on which **Welsh** *sits with a pint, his hands lightly bandaged.* **Girleen** *comes over and sits down beside him.*

Welsh   Girleen.

Girleen   Father. What are ya up to?

Welsh   Just sitting here, now.

Girleen   Oh aye, aye. (*Pause.*) That was a nice sermon at Thomas's today, Father.

Welsh   I didn't see you there, did I?

Girleen   I was at the back a ways. (*Pause.*) Almost made me go crying, them words did.

Welsh   You crying? I've never in all the years heard of you going crying, Girleen. Not at funerals, not at weddings. You didn't even cry when Holland knocked us out of the fecking World Cup.

Girleen   Now and then on me now I go crying, over different things . . .

Welsh   That Packie fecking Bonner. He couldn't save a shot from a fecking cow.

He sips his pint.

Girleen   I'd be saying you've had a few now, Father?

Welsh   Don't you be starting on me now. On top of everybody else.

Girleen   I wasn't starting on ya.

Welsh   Not today of all days.

Girleen   I wasn't starting at all on ya. I do tease you sometimes but that's all I do do.

Welsh   Sometimes, is it? All the time, more like, the same as everybody round here.

Girleen   I do only tease you now and again, and only to camouflage the mad passion I have deep within me for ya . . .

Welsh *gives her a dirty look. She smiles.*

Girleen   No, I'm only joking now, Father.

Welsh   Do ya see?!

Girleen   Ah be taking a joke will ya, Father? It's only cos you're so high-horse and up yourself that you make such an easy target.

Welsh   I'm not so high-horse and up meself.

Girleen   All right you're not so.

Welsh (*pause*)   *Am* I so high-horse and up meself?

Girleen   No, now. Well, no more than most priests.

Welsh   Maybe I am high-horse so. Maybe that's why I don't fit into this town. Although I'd have to have killed half me fecking relatives to fit into this town. Jeez. I thought Leenane was a nice place when first I turned up here, but no. Turns out it's the murder capital of fecking Europe. Did *you* know Coleman had killed his dad on purpose?

Girleen (*lowers head, embarrassed*)   I think I did hear a rumour somewhere along the line . . .

Welsh   A fecking rumour? And you didn't bat an eye or go reporting it?

Girleen   Sure I'm no fecking stool-pigeon and Coleman's dad was always a grumpy oul feck. He did kick me cat Eamonn there once.

Welsh   A fella deserves to die, so, for kicking a cat?

Girleen (*shrugs*)   It depends on the fella. And the cat. But there'd be a lot less cats kicked in Ireland, I'll tell ya, if the fella could rest assured he'd be shot in the head after.

Welsh   You have no morals at all, it seems, Girleen.

Girleen   I have plenty of morals only I don't keep whining on about them like some fellas.

Welsh (*pause*)   Val and Coleman'll kill each other someday if somebody doesn't do something to stop them. It won't be me who stops them anyways. It'll be someone with guts for the job.

He takes out a letter and passes it to **Girleen**.

Welsh   I've written them a little lettereen here, Girleen, would you give it to them next time you see them?

Girleen   Won't you be seeing them soon enough yourself?

Welsh   I won't be. I'm leaving Leenane tonight.

Girleen   Leaving for where?

Welsh   Anywhere. Wherever they send me. Anywhere but here.

Girleen   But why, Father?

Welsh   Ah lots of different reasons, now, but the three slaughterings and one suicide amongst me congregation didn't help.

Girleen   But none of that was your fault, Father.

Welsh   Oh no?

Girleen   And don't you have the under-twelves semi-final tomorrow morning to be coaching?

Welsh   Them bitches have never listened to me advice before. I don't see why they should go starting now. Nobody ever listens to my advice. Nobody ever listens to me at all.

Girleen   I listen to you.

Welsh (*sarcastic*)   Ar that's great comfort.

Girleen *bows her head, hurt.*

Welsh   And you don't listen to me either. How many times have I told you to stop flogging your dad's booze about town, and still you don't?

Girleen   Ah it's just till I save up a few bob, Father, I'm doing that flogging.

Welsh   A few bob for what? To go skittering it away the clubs in Carraroe, and drunk schoolboys pawing at ya.

Girleen   Not at all, Father. I do save it to buy a few nice things out me mam's Freeman's catalogue. They do have an array of . . .

Welsh   To go buying shite, aye. Well, I wish I did have as tough problems in my life as you do in yours, Girleen. It does sound like life's a constant torment for ya.

Girleen *stands up and wrenches* **Welsh**'s *head back by the hair.*

Girleen   If anybody else went talking to me that sarcastic I'd punch them in the fecking eye for them, only if I punched you in the fecking eye you'd probably go crying like a fecking girl!

Welsh   I never asked you to come sitting beside me.

Girleen   Well, I didn't know there was a law against sitting beside ya, although I wish there fecking was one now.

She releases him and starts walking away.

Welsh   I'm sorry for being sarcastic to you, Girleen, about your mam's catalogue and whatnot. I am.

Girleen *stops, pauses, and idles back to the bench.*

Girleen   It's okay.

Welsh   It's only that I'm feeling a bit . . . I don't know . . .

Girleen (*sitting beside him*)   Maudlin.

Welsh   Maudlin. Maudlin is right.

Girleen   Maudlin and lonesome. The maudlin and lonesome Father Walsh. *Welsh.* (*Pause.*) I'm sorry, Father.

Welsh   Nobody ever remembers.

Girleen   It's just Walsh is so close to Welsh, Father.

Welsh   I know it is. I know it is.

Girleen   What's your first name, Father?

Welsh (*pause*)   Roderick.

Girleen *stifles laughter.* **Welsh** *smiles.*

Girleen   Roderick? (*Pause.*) Roderick's a horrible name, Father.

Welsh   I know, and thanks for saying so, Girleen, but you're just trying to boost me spirits now, aren't ya?

Girleen   I'm just being nice to ya now.

Welsh   What kind of a name's Girleen for a girl anyways? What's your proper first name?

Girleen (*cringing*)   Mary.

Welsh (*laughing*)   Mary? And you go laughing at Roderick then?

Girleen   Mary's the name of the mammy of Our Lord, did you ever hear tell of it?

Welsh   I heard of it somewhere along the line.

Girleen   It's the reason she never got anywhere for herself. Fecking Mary.

Welsh   *You'll* be getting somewhere for yourself, Girleen.

Girleen   D'ya think so, now?

Welsh   As tough a get as you are? Going threatening to thump priests? Of course.

Girleen *brushes the hair out of* **Welsh***'s eyes.*

Girleen   I wouldn't have gone thumping you, now, Father.

She gently slaps his cheek.

Maybe a decent slapeen, now.

Welsh *smiles and faces front.* **Girleen** *looks at him, then away, embarrassed.*

Welsh (*pause*)   No, I just came out to have a think about Thomas before I go on me way. Say a little prayer for him.

Girleen   It's tonight you're going?

Welsh   It's tonight, aye. I said to meself I'll stay for Tom's funeral, then that'll be the end of it.

Girleen   But that's awful quick. No one'll have a chance to wish you goodbye, Father.

Welsh   Goodbye, aye, and good riddance to the back of me.

Girleen   Not at all.

Welsh   No?

Girleen   No.

Pause. **Welsh** *nods, unconvinced, and drinks again.*

Girleen   Will you write to me from where you're going and be giving me your new address, Father?

Welsh   I'll try, Girleen, aye.

Girleen   Just so's we can say hello now and then, now.

Welsh   Aye, I'll try.

As he speaks, **Girleen** *manages to stifle tears without him noticing.*

Welsh   This is where he walked in from, d'you know? Poor Tom. Look at as cold and bleak as it is. Do you think it took courage or stupidity for him to walk in, Girleen?

Girleen   Courage.

Welsh   The same as that.

Girleen   And Guinness.

Welsh (*laughing*)   The same as that. (*Pause.*) Look at as sad and as quiet and still.

Girleen   It's more than Thomas has killed himself here down the years, d'you know, Father? Three other fellas walked in here, me mam was telling me.

Welsh   Is that right now?

Girleen   Years and years ago this is. Maybe even famine times.

Welsh   Drowned themselves?

Girleen   This is where they all come.

Welsh   We should be scared of their ghosts so but we're not scared. Why's that?

Girleen   You're not scared because you're pissed to the gills. I'm not scared because . . . I don't know why. One, because you're here, and two, because . . . I don't know. I don't be scared of cemeteries at night either. The opposite of that, I do *like* cemeteries at night.

Welsh   Why, now? Because you're a morbid oul tough?

Girleen (*embarrassed throughout*)   Not at all. I'm not a tough. It's because . . . even if you're sad or something, or lonely or something, you're still better off than them lost in the ground or in the lake, because . . . at least you've got the *chance* of being happy, and even if it's a real little chance, it's more than them dead ones have. And it's not that you're saying 'Hah, I'm better than ye', no, because in the long run it might end up that you have a worse life than ever they had and you'd've been better off as dead as them, there and then. But at least when you're still here there's the *possibility* of happiness, and it's like them dead ones know that, and they're happy for you to have it. They say 'Good luck to ya.' (*Quietly.*) Is the way I see it anyways.

Welsh   You have a million thoughts going on at the back of them big brown eyes of yours.

Girleen   I never knew you did ever notice me big brown eyes. Aren't they gorgeous, now?

Welsh   You'll grow up to be a mighty fine woman one day, Girleen, God bless you.

He drinks again.

Girleen (*quietly, sadly*)   One day, aye. (*Pause.*) I'll be carrying on the road home for meself now, Father. Will you be staying or will you be walking with me?

Welsh   I'll be staying a biteen longer for meself, Girleen. I'll be saying that prayer for poor Thomas, now.

Girleen   It's goodbye for a while so.

Welsh   It is.

Girleen *kisses his cheek and they hug.* **Girleen** *stands.*

Welsh   You'll remember to be giving that letter to Valene and Coleman, now, Girleen?

Girleen   I will. What's in it, Father? It does sound very mysterious. It wouldn't be packed full of condoms for them, would it?

Welsh   It wouldn't at all, now!

Girleen   Cos, you know, Valene and Coleman'd get no use out of them, unless they went using them on a hen.

Welsh   Girleen, now . . .

Girleen   And it'd need to be a blind hen.

Welsh   You do have a terrible mouth on ya.

Girleen   Aye, all the better to . . . no, I won't be finishing that sentence. Did you hear tell of Valene's new hobby, Father? He's been roaming the entirety of Connemara picking up new figurines of the saints for himself, but only ceramic and china ones won't go melting away on him. Thirty-seven of them at last count he has, and only to go tormenting poor Coleman.

Welsh   Them two, they're just odd.

Girleen   They *are* odd. They're the kings of odd. (*Pause.*) See you so, Father.

Welsh   See you so, Girleen. Or Mary, is it?

Girleen   If you let me know where you get to I'll write with how the under-twelves get on tomorrow. It may be in the *Tribune* anyways. Under 'Girl decapitated in football match'.

Welsh *nods, half smiles.* **Girleen** *idles away.*

Welsh   Girleen, now? Thanks for coming sitting next to me. It's meant something to me, it has.

Girleen   Any time, Father. Any time.

Girleen *exits.* **Welsh** *stares out front again.*

Welsh (*quietly*)   No, not any time, Girleen. Not any time.

He finishes his pint, puts the glass down, blesses himself and sits there quietly a moment, thinking. Blackout.

Scene Five

Stage in darkness apart from **Welsh**, *who recites his letter rapidly.*

Welsh   Dear Valene and Coleman, it is Father Welsh here. I am leaving Leenane for good tonight and I wanted to be saying a few words to you, but I won't be preaching at you for why would I be? It has never worked in the past and it won't work now. All I want to do is be pleading with you as a fella

concerned about ye and yere lives, both in this world and the
next, and the next won't be too long away for ye's if ye keep
going on as mad as ye fecking have been. Coleman, I will not
be speaking here about your murdering of your dad, although
obviously it does concern me, both as a priest and as a person
with even the vaguest moral sense, but that is a matter for your
own conscience, although I hope some day you will realise
what you have done and go seeking forgiveness for it, because
let me tell you this, getting your hairstyle insulted is no just
cause to go murdering someone, in fact it's the worst cause I
did ever hear. But I will leave it at that although the same goes
for you, Valene, for your part in your dad's murdering, and
don't go saying you had no part because you did have a part
and a big part. Going lying that it was an accident just to get
your father's money is just as dark a deed as Coleman's deed, if
not more dark, for Coleman's deed was done out of temper
and spite, whereas your deed was done out of being nothing
but a money-grubbing fecking miser with no heart at all, but
I said I would not be preaching at you and I have lost me
thread anyways so I will stop preaching at you and be starting
a new paragraph. (*Pause.*) Like I said, I am leaving tonight, but
I have been thinking about ye non-stop since the night I did
scald me hands there at yeres. Every time the pain does go
through them hands I do think about ye, and let me tell you
this. I would take that pain and pain a thousand times worse,
and bear it with a smile, if only I could restore to ye the love
for each other as brothers ye do so woefully lack, that must
have been there some day. Didn't as gasurs ye love each other?
Or as young men, now? Where did it all go on ye? Don't ye
ever think about it? What I think I think what ye've done is
bury it deep down in ye, under a rack of grudges and hate and
sniping like a pair of fecking oul women. Ye two are like a pair
of fecking oul women, so ye are, arging over fecking Taytos
and stoves and figurines, is an arse-brained argument. But I do
think that yere love is still there under all of that, in fact I'd
go betting everything that's dear to me on it, and may I rot in
hell for ever if I'm wrong. All it is is ye've lived in each other's
pockets the entire of yere lives, and a sad and lonesome
existence it has been, with no women to enter the picture for

either of ye to calm ye down, or anyways not many women or the wrong sort of women, and what's happened the bitterness has gone building up and building up without check, the daily grudges and faults and moans and baby-crimes against each other ye can never seem to step back from and see the love there underneath and forgive each other for. Now, what the point of me letter is, couldn't ye do something about it? Couldn't the both of ye, now, go stepping back and be making a listeen of all the things about the other that do get on yere nerves, and the wrongs the other has done all down through the years that you still hold against him, and be reading them lists out, and be discussing them openly, and be taking a deep breath then and be forgiving each other them wrongs, no matter what they may be? Would that be so awful hard, now? It would for ye two, I know, but couldn't ye just be trying it, now? And if it doesn't work it doesn't work, but at least ye could say ye'd tried and would ye be any worse off? And if ye wouldn't be doing it for yourselves, wouldn't ye be doing it for me, now? For a friend of yeres, who cares about ye, who doesn't want to see ye blowing the brains out of each other, who never achieved anything as a priest in Leenane, in fact the opposite, and who'd see ye two becoming true brothers again as the greatest achievement of his whole time here. Sure it would be bordering on the miraculous. I might be canonised after. (*Pause.*) Valene and Coleman, I'm betting everything on ye. I know for sure there's love there somewheres, it's just a case of ye stepping back and looking for it. I'd be willing to bet me own soul that that love is there, and I know well the odds are stacked against me. They're probably 64,000 to one be this time, but I'd go betting on ye's still, for despite everything, despite yere murder and yere mayhem and yere miserliness that'd tear the teeth out of broken goats, I have faith in ye. You wouldn't be letting me down now, would ye? Yours sincerely, and yours with the love of Christ now, Roderick Welsh.

Pause. **Welsh** *shivers slightly. Blackout.*

Scene Six

Valene's *house. Shotgun back on wall, over shelf full of new ceramic figurines, all marked with a 'V'.* **Coleman**, *in glasses, sits in the armchair left, glass of poteen beside him, perusing another women's magazine.* **Valene** *enters carrying a bag and places his hand on the stove in a number of places. Irritated,* **Coleman** *tries to ignore him.*

Valene   I'm checking. (*Pause.*) It's good to have a little check. (*Pause.*) *I* think it is, d'you know? (*Pause.*) Just a *little* check. D'you know what I mean, like?

After a while more of this, **Valene** *takes some new ceramic figurines out of his bag, which he arranges with the others on the shelf.*

Coleman   Ah for . . .

Valene   Eh?

Coleman   Eh?

Valene   Now then, eh?

Coleman   Uh-huh?

Valene   Eh? Nice, I think. Eh? What do *you* think, Coleman?

Coleman   I think you can go feck yourself.

Valene   No, not feck meself at all, now. Or over to the left a biteen would they look better? Hmm, we'll put the new St Martin over here, so it balances out with the other St Martin over there, so's we have one darkie saint on either side, so it balances out symmetrical, like. (*Pause.*) I'm a great one for shelf arranging I am. It is a skill I did never know I had. (*Pause.*) Forty-six figurines now. I'm sure to be getting into heaven with this many figurines in me house.

Valene *finds his pen and marks up the new figurines.*

Coleman (*pause*)   There's a poor girl born in Norway here with no lips.

Valene (*pause*)   That's old news that lip girl is.

Coleman   That girl'll never be getting kissed. Not with the bare gums on her flapping.

Valene   She's the exact same as you, so, if she'll never be getting kissed, and you've no excuse. You've the full complement of lips.

Coleman   I suppose a million girls you've kissed in your time. Oh aye.

Valene   Nearer two million.

Coleman   Two million, aye. And all of them aunties when you was twelve.

Valene   Not aunties at all. Proper women.

Coleman   Me brother Valentine does be living in his own little dream-world, with the sparrows and the fairies and the hairy little men. Puw-ooh! And the daisy people.

Valene (*pause*)   I hope that's not my poteen.

Coleman   It's not at all your poteen.

Valene   Uh-huh? (*Pause.*) Did you hear the news?

Coleman   I did. Isn't it awful?

Valene   It's a disgrace. It's an outright disgrace, and nothing but. You can't go sending off an entire girls' football team, sure.

Coleman   Not in a semi-fecking-final anyways.

Valene   Not at any time, sure. If you have to send people off you send them off one at a time, for their individual offences. You don't go slinging the lot of them off wholesale, and only seven minutes in, so they go crying home to their mammies.

Coleman   St Josephine's have only got through be default, and nothing but default. If they had any honour they'd not take their place in the final at all and be giving it to us.

Valene   I hope they lose the final.

Coleman   The same as that, *I* hope they lose the final. Sure, with their goalie in a coma they're bound to.

Valene   No, their goalie came out of her coma a while ago there. Intensive care is all she's in now.

Coleman   She was fecking feigning? Getting us expelled from all competitions for no reason at all? I hope she relapses into her coma and dies.

Valene   The same as that, I hope she lapses into her coma and dies. (*Pause.*) Look at us, we're in agreement.

Coleman   We are, I suppose.

Valene   We can agree sometimes.

He snatches the magazine out of **Coleman***'s hands.*

Valene   Except don't go reading me magazines, I've told you, till I've finished reading them.

He sits at the table and flips through the magazine without reading it.
Coleman *fumes.*

Coleman (*standing*)   And don't go . . . don't go tearing them out of me fecking hands, near tore the fingers off me!

Valene   Have these fingers you (*V-sign*) and take them to bed with ya.

Coleman   You're not even reading that *Take a Break.*

Valene   I *am* reading this *Take a Break*, or anyways I'm glancing through this *Take a Break* at me own pace, as a fella's free to do if it's with his own money he goes buying his *Take a Break.*

Coleman   Only women's magazines is all you ever go reading. Sure without doubt it's a fecking gayboy you must be.

Valene   There's a lad here in Bosnia and not only has he no arms but his mammy's just died. (*Mumbles as he reads, then:*) Ah they're only after fecking money, the same as ever.

Coleman   And no fear of you sending that poor no-armed boy any money, ah no.

Valene   They've probably only got him to put his arms behind his back, just to cod ya.

Coleman   It's any excuse for you.

Valene   And I bet his mammy's fine.

Coleman (*pause*)   Get *Bella* if you're getting magazines. *Take a Break*'s nothing but quizzes.

Valene   There's a coupon here for Honey Nut Loops.

Valene *starts carefully tearing out the coupon at the same time as* **Coleman** *quietly takes some Taytos out of a cupboard.*

Coleman   Quizzes and deformed orphans. (*Pause.*) Em, would you let me be having a bag of Taytos, Val? I'm hungry a biteen.

Valene (*looking up. Pause*)   Are you being serious, now?

Coleman   G'wan. I'll owe you for them.

Valene   Put that bag back, now.

Coleman   I'll owe you for them, I'm saying. You can put them on the same bill you've put your melted figurines.

Valene   Put them . . . put them . . . What are you doing, now? Put them Taytos back, I said.

Coleman   Valene, listen to me . . .

Valene   No . . .

Coleman   I'm hungry and I need some Taytos. Didn't I wait till you came back in to ask you, now, and only because I'm honest . . .

Valene   And you've asked me and I've said no. Slinging insults at me Taytos the other week I remember is all you were. I see the boot's on the other foot now.

Coleman   I've asked polite, now, Valene, and feck boots. Three times I've asked polite.

Valene   I know well you've asked polite, Coleman. You've asked awful polite. And what I'm saying to ya, ya can't have any of me fecking Taytos, now!

Coleman   Is that your final word on the subject?

Valene   It *is* me final word on the subject.

Coleman (*pause*)   I won't have any of your Taytos so. (*Pause.*)
I'll just crush them to skitter.

He crushes the crisps to pulp and tosses the packet at **Valene**. **Valene**
darts up and around the table to get at **Coleman**, *during which time*
Coleman *grabs two more packets from the cupboard and holds them
up, one in each hand, threatening to crush them also.*

Coleman   Back off!

Valene *stops dead in his tracks.*

Coleman   Back off or they'll be getting it the same!

Valene (*scared*)   Be leaving me crisps now, Coleman.

Coleman   Be leaving them, is it? When all I wanted was to
go buying one of them and would've paid the full whack, but
oh no.

Valene (*tearfully, choking*)   That's a waste of good food that is,
Coleman.

Coleman   Good food, is it?

Valene   There's Bosnians'd be happy to have them Taytos.

Coleman *opens one of the bags and starts eating just as the front door
bangs open and* **Girleen** *enters, face blotchy, letter in hand.*

Coleman   They *are* good food, d'you know?

Girleen (*in shock throughout*)   Have ye heard the news, now?

Coleman   What news, Girleen? The under-twelves . . . ?

Seeing **Coleman** *distracted,* **Valene** *dives for his neck, trying to get
the crisps off him at the same time. They drag each other to the floor,
rolling and scuffling,* **Coleman** *purposely mashing up the crisps any
chance he gets.* **Girleen** *stares at them a while, then quietly takes a
butcher's knife out of one of the drawers, goes over to them, pulls*
Coleman's *head back by the hair and puts the knife to his neck.*

Valene   Leave Coleman alone, Girleen. What are you doing,
now?

Girleen   I'm breaking ye up.

Coleman (*scared*)   We're broke up.

Valene (*scared*)   We're broke up.

Once the two are separated, **Girleen** *lets* **Coleman** *go and puts the letter on the table, sadly.*

Girleen   There's a letter there Father Welsh wrote ye.

Valene   What does that feck want writing to us?

Coleman   Going moaning again, I'll bet.

Valene *picks the letter up,* **Coleman** *pulls it off him,* **Valene** *pulls it back. They stand reading it together,* **Coleman** *getting bored after a few seconds.* **Girleen** *takes out a heart pendant on a chain and looks at it.*

Girleen   I read it already on ye, coming over. All about the two of ye loving each other as brothers it is.

Coleman (*stifling laughter*)   Wha?

Valene   Father Walsh Welsh's leaving, it looks like.

Coleman   Is it full of moaning, Valene? It is.

Valene   And nothing but moaning. (*Mimicking*) 'Getting your hairstyle insulted is no just cause to go murdering someone, in fact it's the worst cause I did ever hear.'

Coleman (*laughing*)   That was a funny voice.

Girleen   I did order him this heart on a chain out of me mam's Freeman's catalogue. Only this morning it came. I asked him to be writing me with his new address last night, so I could send it on to him. I'd've never've got up the courage to be giving it him to his face. I'd've blushed the heart out of me. Four months I've been saving up to buy it him. All me poteen money. (*Crying*) All me poteen money gone. I should've skittered it away the boys in Carraroe, and not go pinning me hopes on a feck I knew full well I'd never have.

Girleen *cuts the chain in two with the knife.*

Coleman   Don't be cutting your good chain there, Girleen.

Valene Be leaving your chaineen there now, Girleen. That chain looks worth something.

Girleen *tosses the chain in a corner.*

Girleen (*sniffling*) Have you read the letter there, now?

Valene I have. A pile of oul bull.

Girleen I read it to see if he mentioned me. Not a word.

Coleman Just shite is it, Valene? It's not worth reading?

Valene Not at all.

Coleman I'll leave it so, for I've no time for letters. I've never seen the sense in them. They're just writing.

Girleen I did like the bit about him betting his soul on ye. Didn't ye like that bit?

Valene *picks up the broken chain.*

Valene I don't think I understood that bit.

Girleen (*pause*) Father Welsh drowned himself in the lake last night, same place as Tom Hanlon. They dragged his body out this morning. His soul in hell he's talking about, that only ye can save for him. (*Pause.*) You notice he never asked me to go saving his soul. I'd've liked to've saved his soul. I'd've been honoured, but no. (*Crying.*) Only mad drunken pig-shite feck-brained thicks he goes asking.

Shocked, **Coleman** *reads the letter.* **Girleen** *goes to the door.* **Valene** *offers the pendant out to her.*

Valene Your heart, Girleen, be keeping it for yourself.

Girleen (*crying*) Feck me heart. Feck it to hell. Toss it into fecking skitter's the best place for that fecking heart. (*Exiting.*) Not even a word to me!

After **Girleen** *exits,* **Valene** *sits in an armchair, looking at the chain.* **Coleman** *finishes reading the letter, leaves it on the table and sits in the opposite armchair.*

Valene Did you read it?

Coleman I did.

Valene (*pause*) Isn't it sad about him?

Coleman It *is* sad. Very sad.

Valene (*pause*) Will we be trying for ourselves? To get along, now?

Coleman We will.

Valene There's no harm in trying.

Coleman No harm at all, sure.

Valene (*pause*) Poor Father Welsh Walsh Welsh.

Coleman Welsh.

Valene Welsh. (*Pause.*) I wonder why he did it?

Coleman I suppose he must've been upset o'er something.

Valene I suppose. (*Pause.*) This is a pricey chain. (*Pause.*) We'll be giving it back to her next time we see her. She's only shocked now.

Coleman Aye. She's not in her right mind at all. She did hurt me hair when she tugged at it too, d'you know?

Valene It did look like it hurt.

Coleman It did hurt.

Valene (*pause*) Father Welsh going topping himself does put arging o'er Taytos into perspective anyways.

Coleman It does.

Valene Eh?

Coleman It does.

Valene Aye. Awful perspective. Awful perspective.

Coleman (*pause*) Did you see 'Roderick' his name is?

Valene (*snorts*) I did.

Coleman (*pause. Seriously*) We shouldn't laugh.

Valene nods. *Both pull serious faces. Blackout.*

Scene Seven

Room tidier. **Welsh**'s *letter pinned to the foot of the crucifix.* **Valene** *and* **Coleman** *enter dressed in black, having just attended* **Welsh**'s *funeral,* **Coleman** *carrying a small plastic bag full of sausage rolls and vol-au-vents. He sits at the table.* **Valene** *opens his poteen biscuit tin.*

Valene   That's that, then.

Coleman   That's that, aye. That's Father Welsh gone.

Valene   A good do.

Coleman   Aye. It's often a good do when it's a priest they're sticking away.

He empties his bag onto table.

Valene   You didn't have to go nabbing a whole bagful, now, Coleman.

Coleman   Didn't they offer, sure?

Valene   But a whole bagful, I'm saying.

Coleman   It'd have only gone to waste, and sure a bagful won't be going very far between us.

Valene   Between us?

Coleman   Of course between us.

Valene   Ohh.

They both eat a little.

These are nice vol-au-vents.

Coleman   They *are* nice vol-au-vents.

Valene   You can't say the Catholic Church doesn't know how to make a nice vol-au-vent, now.

Coleman   It's their best feature. And their sausage rolls aren't bad either, although they probably only buy them in.

Valene (*pause*)   Em, would you be having a glass of poteen with me, Coleman?

Coleman (*shocked*) I would, now. If you can spare a drop, like.

Valene I can easy spare a drop.

Valene *pours two glasses, one bigger than the other, thinks about it, then gives* **Coleman** *the bigger.*

Coleman Thank you, Valene. Sure we have our own little feasteen now.

Valene We do.

Coleman D'you remember when as gasurs we did used to put the blankets o'er the gap between our beds and hide under them like a tent it was o'er us, and go having a feasteen of oul jammy sandwiches then?

Valene That was you and Mick Dowd used to go camping in the gap between our beds. You'd never let me be in with yous at all. Ye used to step on me head if I tried to climb into that camp with you. I still remember it.

Coleman Mick Dowd, was it? I don't remember that at all, now. I did think it was you.

Valene Half me childhood you spent stepping on me head, and for no reason. And d'you remember when you pinned me down and sat across me on me birthday and let the stringy spit dribble out your gob and let down and down it dribble till it landed in me eye then?

Coleman I remember it well, Valene, and I'll tell you this. I did mean to suck that spit back up just before it got to your eye, but what happened I lost control o'er it.

Valene And on me birthday.

Coleman (*pause*) I do apologise for dribbling in your eye and I do apologise for stepping on your head, Valene. On Father Welsh's soul I apologise.

Valene I do accept your apology so.

Coleman   Although plenty of times as a gasur I remember you dropping stones on me head while I was asleep and big stones.

Valene   Only in retaliation them stones ever was.

Coleman   Retaliation or not. Waking up to stones dropped on ya is awful frightening for a small child. And retaliation doesn't count anyways if it's a week later. It's only then and there retaliation does apply.

Valene   I do apologise for dropping stones on you so. (*Pause.*) For your brain never did recover from them injuries, did it, Coleman?

Coleman *stares at* **Valene** *a second, then smiles.* **Valene** *smiles also.*

Valene   This is a great oul game, this is, apologising. Father Welsh wasn't too far wrong.

Coleman   I hope Father Welsh isn't in hell at all. I hope he's in heaven.

Valene   *I* hope he's in heaven.

Coleman   Or purgatory at worst.

Valene   Although if he's in hell at least he'll have Tom Hanlon to speak to.

Coleman   So it won't be as if he doesn't know anybody.

Valene   Aye. And the fella off *Alias Smith and Jones.*

Coleman   Is the fella off *Alias Smith and Jones* in hell?

Valene   He is. Father Welsh was telling me.

Coleman   The blond one.

Valene   No, the other one.

Coleman   He was good, the other one.

Valene   He was the best one.

Coleman   It's always the best ones go to hell. Me, probably straight to heaven I'll go, even though I blew the head off poor

Dad. So long as I go confessing to it anyways. That's the good thing about being Catholic. You can shoot your dad in the head and it doesn't even matter at all.

Valene   Well, it matters a little bit.

Coleman   It matters a little bit but not a big bit.

Valene (*pause*)   Did you see Girleen crying her eyes out, the funeral?

Coleman   I did.

Valene   Poor Girleen. And her mam two times has had to drag her screaming from the lake at night, did you hear, there where Father Walsh jumped, and her just standing there, staring.

Coleman   She must've liked Father Welsh or something.

Valene   I suppose she must've. (*Taking out* **Girleen**'s *chain.*) She wouldn't take her chaineen back at all. She wouldn't hear tell of it. I'll put it up here with his letter to us.

He attaches the chain to the cross, so the heart rests on the letter, which he gently smoothes out.

It's the mental they'll be putting Girleen in before long if she carries on.

Coleman   Sure it's only a matter of time.

Valene   Isn't that sad?

Coleman   Awful sad. (*Pause. Shrugging.*) Ah well.

He eats another vol-au-vent. **Valene** *remembers something, fishes in the pockets of his jacket, takes out two ceramic figurines, places them on the shelf, uncaps his pen almost automatically, thinks better of marking them as before, and puts the pen away.*

Coleman   I think I'm getting to like vol-au-vents now. I think I'm developing a taste for them. We ought to go to more funerals.

Valene   They do have them at weddings too.

Coleman   Do they? Who'll next be getting married round here so? Girleen I would used to have said, as pretty as she is, only she'll probably have topped herself before ever she gets married.

Valene   *Me* probably'll be the next one getting married, as handsome as I am. Did you see today all the young nuns eyeing me?

Coleman   Who'd go marrying you, sure? Even that no-lipped girl in Norway'd turn you down.

Valene (*pause. Angrily*)   See, I'm stepping back now . . . I'm stepping back, like Father Walsh said, and I'm forgiving ya, insulting me.

Coleman (*sincerely*)   Oh . . . oh, I'm sorry now, Valene. I'm sorry. It just slipped out on me without thinking.

Valene   No harm done so, if only an accident it was.

Coleman   It *was* an accident. Although remember you did insult me there earlier, saying I was brain-damaged be stones as a gasur, and I didn't even pull you up on it.

Valene   I apologise for saying you was brain-damaged as a gasur so.

Coleman   No apology was necessary, Valene, and I have saved you the last vol-au-venteen on top of it.

Valene   You have that last vol-au-vent, Coleman. I'm not overly keen on vol-au-vents.

Coleman *nods in thanks and eats the vol-au-vent.*

Valene   Weren't them young nuns lovely today now, Coleman?

Coleman   They was lovely nuns.

Valene   They must've known Father Welsh from nun college or something.

Coleman   I'd like to touch them nuns both upstairs and downstairs, so I would. Except for the fat one on the end.

Valene   She was a horror and she knew.

Coleman If Dad was there today he'd've just gone screaming at them nuns.

Valene Why *did* Dad used to go screaming at nuns, Coleman?

Coleman I don't have an idea at all why he used to scream at nuns. He must've had a bad experience with nuns as a child.

Valene If you hadn't blown the brains out of Dad we could ask him outright.

Coleman *stares at him sternly.*

Valene No, I'm not saying anything, now. I'm calm, I've stepped back, and I'm saying this quietly and without any spite at all, but you know well that that wasn't right, Coleman, shooting Dad in the head on us. In your heart anyways you know.

Coleman (*pause*) I *do* know it wasn't right. Not only in me heart but in me head and in me everywhere. I was wrong for shooting Dad. I was dead wrong. And I'm sorry for it.

Valene And I'm sorry for sitting you down and making you sign your life away, Coleman. It was the only way at the time I could think of punishing ya. Well, I could've let you go to jail but I didn't want you going to jail and it wasn't out of miserliness that I stopped you going to jail. It was more out of I didn't want all on me own to be left here. I'd've missed ya. (*Pause.*) From this day on . . . from this day on, this house and everything in this house is half yours again, Coleman.

Touched, **Coleman** *offers his hand out and they shake, embarrassed. Pause.*

Valene Is there any other confessions we have to get off our chests, now we're at it?

Coleman There must be millions. (*Pause.*) Crushing your crisps to skitter, Valene, I'm sorry for.

Valene I forgive you for it. (*Pause.*) Do you remember that holiday in Lettermullen as gasurs we had, and you left your cowboy stagecoach out in the rain that night and next morning it was gone and Mam and Dad said, 'Oh it must've been hijacked be Indians.' It wasn't hijacked be Indians. I'd got up early and pegged it in the sea.

Coleman (*pause*)   I did love that cowboy stagecoach.

Valene   I know you did, and I'm sorry for it.

Coleman (*pause*)   That string of gob I dribbled on you on your birthday. I didn't try to suck it back up at all. I wanted it to hit your eye and I was glad. (*Pause.*) And I'm sorry for it.

Valene   Okay. (*Pause.*) Maureen Folan did once ask me to ask you if you wanted to see a film at the Claddagh Palace with her, and she'd've driven ye and paid for dinner too, and from the tone of her voice it sounded like you'd've been on a promise after, but I never passed the message onto ya, out of nothing but pure spite.

Coleman   Sure that's no great loss, Valene. Maureen Folan looks like a thin-lipped ghost, with the hairstyle of a frightened red ape.

Valene   But on a promise you'd've been.

Coleman   On a promise or no. That was nothing at all to go confessing. Okay, it's my go. I'm winning.

Valene   What d'you mean, you're winning?

Coleman (*thinking*)   Do you remember your Ker-Plunk game?

Valene   I *do* remember me Ker-Plunk game.

Coleman   It wasn't Liam Hanlon stole all them marbles out of your Ker-Plunk game at all, it was me.

Valene   What did you want me Ker-Plunk marbles for?

Coleman   I went slinging them at the swans in Galway. I had a great time.

Valene   That ruined me Ker-Plunk. You can't play Ker-Plunk without marbles. And, sure, that was *both* of ours Ker-Plunk.

That was just cutting off your nose to spite your face, Coleman.

Coleman   I know it was and I'm sorry, Valene. Your go now. (*Pause.*) You're too slow. D'you remember when we had them backward children staying for B & B, and they threw half your *Spider Man* comics in on the fire? They didn't. D'you know who did? I did. I only blamed them cos they were too daft to arg.

Valene   They was good *Spider Man* comics, Coleman. Spider Man went fighting Doctor Octopus in them comics.

Coleman   And I'm sorry for it. Your go. (*Pause.*) You're too slow . . .

Valene   Hey . . . !

Coleman   D'you remember when Pato Dooley beat the skitter out of you when he was twelve and you was twenty, and you never knew the reason why? I knew the reason why. I did tell him you'd called his dead mammy a hairy whore.

Valene   With a fecking chisel that Pato Dooley beat me up that day! Almost had me fecking eye out!

Coleman   I think Pato must've liked his mammy or something. (*Pause.*) I'm awful sorry for it, Valene.

He burps lazily.

Valene   You do sound it!

Coleman   Shall I be having another go?

Valene   I did pour a cup of piss in a pint of lager you drank one time, Coleman. Aye, and d'you know what, now? You couldn't even tell the differ.

Coleman (*pause*)   When was this, now?

Valene   When you was seventeen, this was. D'you remember that month you were laid up in hospital with bacterial tonsilitis. Around then it was. (*Pause.*) And I'm sorry for it, Coleman.

Coleman   I do take your poteen out its box each week, drink the half of it and fill the rest back up with water. Ten years this has been going on. You haven't tasted full-strength poteen since nineteen eighty-fecking-three.

Valene (*drinks. Pause*)   But you're sorry for it.

Coleman   I suppose I'm sorry for it, aye. (*Mumbling.*) Making me go drinking piss, and not just anybody's piss but *your* fecking piss . . .

Valene (*angrily*)   But you're sorry for it, you're saying?!

Coleman   I'm sorry for it, aye! I'm fecking sorry for it! Haven't I said?!

Valene   That's okay, so, if you're sorry for it, although you don't sound fecking sorry for it.

Coleman   You can kiss me fecking arse so, Valene, if you don't . . . I'm taking a step back now, so I am. (*Pause.*) I'm sorry for watering your poteen down all these years, Valene. I am, now.

Valene   Good-oh. (*Pause.*) Is it your go now or is it mine?

Coleman   I think it might be your go, Valene.

Valene   Thank you, Coleman. D'you remember when Alison O'Hoolihan went sucking that pencil in the playground that time, and ye were to go dancing the next day, but somebody nudged that pencil and it got stuck in her tonsils on her, and be the time she got out of hospital she was engaged to the doctor who wrenched it out for her and wouldn't be giving you a fecking sniffeen. Do you remember, now?

Coleman   I do remember.

Valene   That was me nudged that pencil, and it wasn't an accident at all. Pure jealous I was.

Pause. **Coleman** *throws his sausage rolls in* **Valene**'*s face and dives over the table for his neck.* **Valene** *dodges the attack.*

Valene   And I'm sorry for it! I'm sorry for it! (*Pointing at letter.*) Father Welsh! Father Welsh!

Valene *fends* **Coleman** *off. They stand staring at each other,* **Coleman** *seething.*

Coleman   Eh?!

Valene   Eh?

Coleman   I did fecking love Alison O'Hoolihan! We may've been married today if it hadn't been for that fecking pencil!

Valene   What was she doing sucking it the pointy-end inwards anyways? She was looking for trouble!

Coleman   And she fecking found it with you! That pencil could've killed Alison O'Hoolihan!

Valene   And I'm sorry for it, I said. What are you doing pegging good sausage rolls at me? Them sausage rolls cost money. You were supposed to have taken a step back and went calming yourself, but you didn't, you just flew off the handle. Father Welsh's soul'll be roasting now because of you.

Coleman   Leave Father Welsh's soul out of it. This is about you sticking pencils down poor girls' gobs on them.

Valene   That pencil is water under a bridge and I've apologised wholehearted for that pencil. (*Sits down.*) And she had boss-eyes anyways.

Coleman   She didn't have boss-eyes! She had nice eyes!

Valene   Well, there was something funny about them.

Coleman   She had nice brown eyes.

Valene   Oh aye. (*Pause.*) Well, it's your go now, Coleman. Try and top that one for yourself. Heh.

Coleman   Try and top that one, is it?

Valene   It is.

Coleman *thinks for a moment, smiles slightly, then sits back down.*

Coleman I've taken a step back now.

Valene I can see you've taken a step back.

Coleman I'm pure calm now. It does be good to get things off your chest.

Valene It *does* be good. I'm glad that pencil-nudging's off me chest. I can sleep nights now.

Coleman Is it a relief to ya?

Valene It *is* a relief to me. (*Pause.*) What have you got cooking up?

Coleman I have one and I'm terrible sorry for it. Oh terrible sorry I am.

Valene It won't be near as good as me pencilling poor boss-eyed Alison, whatever it is.

Coleman Ah I suppose you're right, now. My one's only a weeny oul one. D'you remember you always thought it was Mairtin Hanlon snipped the ears off of poor Lassie, now?

Valene (*confidently*) I don't believe you at all. You're only making it up now, see.

Coleman It wasn't wee Mairtin at all. D'you know who it was, now?

Valene Me arse was it you. You'll have to be doing better than that, now, Coleman.

Coleman To the brookeen I dragged him, me scissors in hand, and him whimpering his fat gob off 'til the deed was done and he dropped down dead with not a fecking peep out of that whiny fecking dog.

Valene D'you see, it doesn't hurt me at all when you go making up lies. You don't understand the rules, Coleman. It does have to be true, else it's just plain daft. You can't go claiming credit for snipping the ears off a dog when you didn't lay a finger on that dog's ears, and the fecking world knows.

Coleman (*pause*) Is it evidence, so, you're after?

Valene   It *is* evidence I'm after, aye. Go bring me evidence you did cut the ears off me dog. And be quick with that evidence.

Coleman   I won't be quick at all. I will take me time.

He slowly gets up and ambles to his room, closing its door behind him. **Valene** *waits patiently, giving a worried laugh. After a ten-second pause,* **Coleman** *ambles back on, carrying a slightly wet brown paper bag. He pauses at the table a moment for dramatic effect, slowly opens the bag, pulls out a dog's big fluffy black ear, lays it on top of* **Valene***'s head, takes out the second ear, pauses, places that on* **Valene***'s head also, puts the empty bag down on the table, smoothes it out, then sits down in the armchair left.* **Valene** *has been staring out into space all the while, dumbstruck. He tilts his head so that the ears fall down onto the table, and he stares at them a while.* **Coleman** *picks up* **Valene***'s felt-tip pen, brings it over and lays it on the table.*

Coleman   There's your little peneen, now, Val. Why don't you mark them dog's ears with your V, so we'll be remembering who they belong to.

He sits back down in the armchair.

And do you want to hear something else, Valene? I'm sorry for cutting off them dog's ears. With all me fecking heart I'm sorry, oh aye, because I've tooken a step back now, look at me . . .

He half laughs through his nose. **Valene** *gets up, stares blankly at* **Coleman** *a moment, goes to the cupboard right and, with his back to* **Coleman***, pulls the butcher's knife out of it. In the same brief second* **Coleman** *stands, pulls the shotgun down from above the stove and sits down with it.* **Valene** *turns, knife ready. The gun is pointed directly at him.* **Valene** *wilts slightly, thinks about it a moment, regains his courage and his anger, and slowly approaches* **Coleman***, raising the knife.*

Coleman (*surprised, slightly scared*)   What are you doing, now, Valene?

Valene (*blankly*)   Oh not a thing am I doing, Coleman, other than killing ya.

Coleman   Be putting that knife back in that drawer, you.

Valene   No, I'll be putting it in the head of you, now.

Coleman   Don't you see me gun?

Valene   Me poor fecking Lassie, who never hurt a flea.

He has gotten all the way up to **Coleman**, *so that the barrel of the gun is touching his chest. He raises the knife to its highest point.*

Coleman   What are you doing, now? Stop it.

Valene   I'll stop it, all right . . .

Coleman   Father Welsh's soul, Valene. Father Wel—

Valene   Father Welsh's soul me fecking arse! Father Welsh's soul didn't come into play when you hacked me dog's ears off him and kept them in a bag!

Coleman   Ar that was a year ago. How does that apply?

Valene   Be saying goodbye to the world, you, ya feck!

Coleman   *You'll* have to be saying goodbye to the world too, so, because I'll be bringing you with me.

Valene   Do I look like I mind that at all, now?

Coleman (*pause*)   Er er, wait wait wait, now . . .

Valene   Wha . . . ?

Coleman   Look at me gun. Look at me gun where it's going, do ya see. . . ?

Coleman *slides the gun away and down from* **Valene***'s chest till it points directly at the door of the stove.*

Valene (*pause*)   Be pointing that gun away from me stove, now.

Coleman   I won't be. Stab away, now. It's your stove it'll be'll be going with me instead of ya.

Valene   Leave . . . what . . . ? That was a three-hundred-pound stove now, Coleman . . .

Coleman   I know well it was.

Valene   Be leaving it alone. That's just being sly, that is.

Coleman   Be backing off you with that knife, you sissy-arse.

Valene (*tearfully*)   You're not a man at all, pointing guns at stoves.

Coleman   I don't care if I am or I'm not. Be backing off, I said.

Valene   You're just a . . . you're just a . . .

Coleman   Eh?

Valene   Eh?

Coleman   Eh?

Valene   You're not a man at all, you.

Coleman   Be backing away now, you, crybaby. Be taking a step back for yourself. Eheh.

Valene (*pause*)   I'm backing away now, so I am.

Coleman   That'd be the best thing, aye.

Valene *slowly retreats, lays the knife on the table and sits down there sadly, gently stroking his dog's ears.* **Coleman** *is still pointing the gun at the stove door. He shakes his head slightly.*

Coleman   I can't believe you raised a knife to me. No, I can't believe you raised a knife to your own brother.

Valene   You raised a knife to me own dog and raised a gun to our own father, did a lot more damage than a fecking knife, now.

Coleman   No, I can't believe it. I can't believe you raised a knife to me.

Valene   Stop going on about raising a knife, and be pointing that gun away from me fecking stove, now, in case it does go off be accident.

Coleman   Be accident, is it?

Valene   Is the safety catch on that gun, now?

Coleman   The safety catch, is it?

Valene   Aye, the safety catch! The safety catch! Is it ten million times I have to be repeating meself?

Coleman   The safety catch, uh-huh . . .

He jumps to his feet, points the gun down at the stove and fires, blowing the right-hand side apart. **Valene** *falls to his knees in horror, his face in his hands.* **Coleman** *cocks the gun again and blows the left-hand side apart also, then nonchalantly sits back down.*

Coleman   No, the safety catch isn't on at all, Valene. Would you believe it?

Pause. **Valene** *is still kneeling there, dumbstruck.*

Coleman   And I'll tell you another thing . . .

He suddenly jumps up again and, holding the shotgun by the barrel, starts smashing it violently into the figurines, shattering them to pieces and sending them flying around the room until not a single one remains standing. **Valene** *screams throughout. After* **Coleman** *has finished he sits again, the gun across his lap.* **Valene** *is still kneeling. Pause.*

Coleman   And don't go making out that you didn't deserve it, because we both know full well that you did.

Valene (*numbly*)   You've broken all me figurines, Coleman.

Coleman   I have. Did you see me?

Valene   And you've blown me stove to buggery.

Coleman   This is a great gun for blowing holes in things.

Valene (*standing*)   And now you do have no bullets left in that great gun.

He lazily picks the knife back up and approaches **Coleman***. But as he does so* **Coleman** *opens the barrel of the gun, tosses away the spent cartridges, fishes in his pocket, comes out with a clenched fist that may or may not contain another cartridge, shows the fist to* **Valene** *. . .*

Valene   There's no bullet in that hand! There's no bullet in that hand!

. . . and loads, or pretends to load, the bullet into the gun, without **Valene** *or the audience at any time knowing if there is a bullet or not.* **Coleman** *snaps the barrel shut and lazily points it at* **Valene**'*s head.*

Coleman *cocks the gun. Long, long pause.*

Valene   I want to kill you, Coleman.

Coleman   Ar, don't be saying that, now, Val.

Valene (*sadly*)   It's true, Coleman. I want to kill you.

Coleman (*pause*)   Try so.

Pause. **Valene** *turns the knife around and around in his hand, staring at* **Coleman** *all the while, until his head finally droops and he returns the knife to the drawer.* **Coleman** *uncocks the gun, stands, and lays it down on the table, staying near it.* **Valene** *idles to the stove and touches the letter pinned above it.*

Valene   Father Welsh is burning in hell, now, because of our fighting.

Coleman   Well, did we ask him to go betting his soul on us? No. And, sure, it's pure against the rules for priests to go betting anyways, never minding with them kinds of stakes. Sure a fiver would've been overdoing it on us, let alone his soul. And what's wrong with fighting anyways? I do like a good fight. It does show you care, fighting does. That's what oul sissy Welsh doesn't understand. Don't you like a good fight?

Valene   I *do* like a good fight, the same as that. Although I don't like having me dog murdered on me, and me fecking dad murdered on me.

Coleman   And I'm sorry for your dog and Dad, Valene. I *am* sorry. Truly I'm sorry. And nothing to do with Father Welsh's letter is this at all. From me own heart this is. The same goes for your stove and your poor figurines too. Look at them. That was pure temper, that was. Although, admit it, you asked for that stove and them figurines.

Valene   You never fecking stop, you. (*Pause.*) *Are* you sorry, Coleman?

Coleman   I am, Valene.

Valene (*pause*)   Maybe Father Walsh's Welsh's soul'll be all right so.

Coleman   Maybe it will, now. Maybe it will.

Valene   He wasn't such a bad fella.

Coleman   He wasn't.

Valene   He wasn't a great fella, but he wasn't a bad fella.

Coleman   Aye. (*Pause.*) He was a *middling* fella.

Valene   He was a *middling* fella.

Coleman (*pause*)   I'm going out for a drink for meself. Will you be coming with me?

Valene   Aye, in a minute now I'll come.

Coleman *goes to the front door.* **Valene** *looks over the smashed figurines sadly.*

Coleman   I'll help you be clearing your figurines up when I get back, Valene. Maybe we can glue some of them together. Do you still have your superglue?

Valene   I do have me superglue, although I think the top's gone hard.

Coleman   Aye, that's the trouble with superglue.

Valene   Ah, the house insurance'll cover me figurines anyways. As well as me stove.

Coleman   Oh . . .

Valene (*pause*)   What, oh?

Coleman   Do you remember a couple of weeks ago there when you asked me did I go stealing your insurance money and I said no, I paid it in for you?

Valene   I do remember. .

Coleman (*pause*)   I didn't pay it in at all. I pocketed the lot of it, pissed it up a wall.

Valene, *seething, darts for the knife drawer.* **Coleman** *dashes out through the front door, slamming it behind him.* **Valene** *tosses the knife away, darts back to the gun and brings it to the door.* **Coleman** *is long gone. Gun in hand,* **Valene** *stands there, shaking with rage, almost in tears. After a while he begins to calm down, taking deep breaths. He looks down at the gun in his hands a moment, then gently opens the barrel to see if* **Coleman** *had really loaded it earlier. He had.* **Valene** *takes the cartridge out.*

Valene   He'd've fecking shot me too. He'd've shot his own fecking brother! On top of his dad! On top of me stove!

He tosses the gun and cartridge away, rips **Father Welsh**'s *letter off the cross, knocking* **Girleen**'s *chain onto the floor, brings the letter back to the table and takes out a box of matches.*

Valene   And you, you whiny fecking priest. Do I need your soul hovering o'er me the rest of me fecking life? How could anybody be getting on with that feck?

He strikes a match and lights the letter, which he glances over as he holds up. After a couple of seconds, the letter barely singed, he blows the flames out and looks at it on the table, sighing.

(*Quietly.*) I'm too fecking kind-hearted is my fecking trouble.

He returns to the cross and pins the chain and letter back onto it, smoothing the letter out. He puts on his jacket, checks it for loose change and goes to the front door.

Well, I won't be buying the fecker a pint anyways. I'll tell you that for nothing, Father Welsh Walsh Welsh.

Valene *glances back at the letter a second, sadly, looks down at the floor, then exits. Lights fade, with one light lingering on the crucifix and letter a half-second longer than the others.*

Notes

page

5 *poteen*: an Irish alcoholic drink. It is usually distilled from potatoes and is extremely potent. Until the late 1990s, it was illegal to sell or brew poteen in Ireland. The fact that the three male characters drink it, and that Girleen sells it, shows that Leenane is a place in which the rule of law is not respected.

5 *fecking*: Irish slang, roughly equivalent to the Standard English 'fucking'. Note, however, that the word 'feck' is never used to refer to sexual intercourse and that 'feck' is not thought to be as crude a word as 'fuck'. It is often assumed that the word 'feck' is an Irish mispronunciation of 'fuck'. In fact, it probably comes from the Elizabethan English 'fecks', meaning 'in faith' (as in Shakespeare's *The Winter's Tale*, I, II, 171, 'I' fecks!').

6 *Maryjohnny*: Maryjohhny Rafferty is a character from *A Skull in Connemara*, the second play in *The Leenane Trilogy*. Viewers of that play will know that Maryjohhny is greedy and self-absorbed, so Coleman's frustration with her seems merited.

6 *vol-au-vent*: a very small, light pastry usually filled with meat or fish. The term is taken from French, and literally means 'flight in the wind'.

6 *biteen*: the suffix *-een* is used as a diminutive in Hiberno-English speech. It can therefore suggest that something is small. Hence, 'biteen' would mean something like 'a little bit'. But it is also sometimes used to express affection, as discussed in the note to p. 13 below.

7 *ye're Dad*: In Hiberno-English speech, the word 'ye' is sometimes used as a plural of 'you'. Welsh is using *ye're* as the possessive plural form of that word – he literally means 'the father of you both'. Welsh is the only

character in McDonagh's plays to use the word 'ye' in this way, which may suggest that his accent is different from that of the other characters.

7   *tech*: short for 'technical college'. Traditionally, these were secondary schools that aimed to prepare students for a trade rather than a profession or university, though the distinction no longer applies.

8   *Tom Hanlon*: another character from *A Skull in Connemara*. Tom is the local police officer. In *Skull*, he is convinced that Mick Dowd (see note to p. 9 below) has murdered his wife. Tom attempts to fabricate the evidence needed to convict Mick, but is unsuccessful in doing so. We learn in Scene Two that Tom has committed suicide, presumably in response to the events in *Skull*.

8   *Mairtin*: also a character in *Skull*, and the brother of Tom. The relationship between Tom and Mairtin is rather similar to that of Valene and Coleman. Mairtin and Tom fight constantly and seem to despise each other, yet as is evident from Mairtin's reaction to news of his brother's death (see p. 28), there is a strong bond between the pair. This characterisation can be seen as another example of Coleman's suggestion at the end of the play that fighting between brothers 'does show you care'.

8   *Lassie*: Valene named his dog after the fictional collie that starred in many American films and television shows from the 1940s onwards.

8   *Agin*: the word 'against' is sometimes pronounced 'agin' (to rhyme with 'a bin') in Hiberno-English speech.

9   *Maureen Folan and Mick Dowd*: Maureen Folan is the eponymous heroine of *The Beauty Queen of Leenane*, the first part of *The Leenane Trilogy*. At the conclusion of that play, Maureen beats her mother Mag to death with a poker, but persuades an inquest that Mag died as a result of falling down a hill. Mick Dowd is the protagonist of *A Skull in Connemara*, and is suspected of having killed his wife – though it is never made clear

whether he is guilty of that crime.

9   *Pegging*: an Irish colloquialism, meaning 'to throw'.

9   *codding*: lying, joking or teasing. A Hiberno-English word of uncertain origin.

10   *polis*: a colloquial pronunciation of 'police'.

10   *Hill Street Blues*: an American television programme. Set in an unnamed police precinct in the United States, it was one of the most popular series on British and Irish television during the 1980s.

10   *Woman's Own*: a weekly magazine, published in the UK but also available in Ireland. As the title suggests, it is directed towards a female audience, and usually includes articles on lifestyle issues, health, fashion and celebrities.

11   *Abusing five-year-olds*: Coleman is referring to the widespread abuse of children in Ireland by Catholic clergy. The first Irish person to declare publicly that he had been sexually abused by a priest did so in 1995, only two years before *The Lonesome West* premiered. In subsequent years, it emerged that thousands of people had been victims of physical and sexual abuse by Catholic clergy, over many decades – and that the Catholic hierarchy had covered up those abuses, moving priests from one parish to another rather than reporting their crimes to the police.

11   *I don't think you should be telling me what people be confessing*: confession is one of the sacraments of the Catholic Church. A Catholic may confess his or her sins to a priest, who will recommend an appropriate penance and grant absolution. One of the fundamental features of the sacrament is the Seal of Confession: priests are forbidden to reveal the sins of a person who has confessed to them. Father Walsh has therefore broken one of the major rules of his church, illustrating further that he is indeed a 'shite' priest. See also the note to p. 30.

11   *Montgomery Clift*: Coleman is probably referring to the 1953 Alfred Hitchcock film *I Confess*, in which the

American actor Montgomery Clift plays a Catholic
priest who is forced to choose between breaking the
Seal of Confession and being convicted of a crime that
he did not commit.

12   *them gobshites*: the word 'gobshite' is a highly insulting
term in Hiberno-English, combining the words 'gob',
meaning 'mouth' or 'spit', with the regionalised
pronunciation of the word 'shit'. Coleman uses the
word 'them' to mean 'those' here.

12   *pegging the first stone*: he may not realise that he is doing
so, but Welsh is paraphrasing John 8:7: 'Let he who is
without sin cast the first stone.'

12   *Connaught*: one of the four provinces of Ireland, located
on the island's west coast and including the county of
Galway, where this play is set.

13   *red cards*: in sport a red card is used when a player has
committed an infringement of the rules. If the referee
deems the infringement to be very serious, he may
decide that the player should be sent off – which he will
signify by brandishing a red card in the direction of the
player.

13   *St Angela's*: there is a primary school called St Angela's
in Castlebar, a town in Connaught that is about 50
kilometres from Leenane.

13   *Girleen*: her real name is Mary; Girleen is a nickname.
As stated in the note to p. 6, the suffix-een is a
diminutive. Hence, 'Girleen' would mean something
like 'little girl'. But the appearance of '-een' at the end
of a word can also be a term of endearment, so
'Girleen' could also mean something like 'lovely girl'.
Upon first appearance Girleen seems neither lovely nor
little, but we'll learn during the play that the nickname
is not entirely inappropriate.

13   *Father Welsh Walsh Welsh*: this is a running joke from the
first two plays in *The Leenane Trilogy*, and another sign of
Father Welsh's low status in his community. The
people of Leenane constantly get Father Welsh's name
wrong, believing that his surname is the far more

common 'Walsh'.

13   *Don't be picking me up*: Girleen means 'don't correct me'.

13   *EC*: the European Community, the name for the European Union (of which Ireland is a part) prior to 1992.

14   *Taytos*: Taytos are a brand of crisps (potato chips), manufactured in Ireland. As is implied on the next page, Taytos are somewhat cheaper than other brands.

14   *flogging*: in this context, 'to flog' is a slang word, meaning 'to sell'.

15   *Be stopping*: in Hiberno-English, the imperative is sometimes formed by using the word 'be', followed by the present participle of a verb. 'Be stopping!' means the same thing as 'Stop!', though there is a slight difference in emphasis: 'be stopping' might be construed as a demand to come to a gradual conclusion, whereas 'stop' means to conclude something immediately. Elsewhere in the play, the construction 'be' followed by the participle is used to form a kind of present continual tense, as in 'don't you be starting on me again' on p. 10 – that is, the construction is used to describe an ongoing process that is occurring in the present. This is a literal translation of a verb tense that exists in Irish but which is absent from the English language.

16   *Ye's two*: here 'ye's' is a plural form of the word 'you'. Again, Welsh is the only character to use the word in this way.

18   *same differ*: 'difference' is sometimes shortened to 'differ' in Hiberno-English.

19   *McCoys*: another brand of crisps. Unlike Tayto, they are imported to Ireland from the UK and, as Coleman says, they 'have grooves' – that is, they are crinkle-cut.

19   *seventeen pee*: before 2001, the unit of currency in Ireland was the Irish pound or 'punt', one pound equalled one hundred pence. 17p. is worth about 20 cents in the euro currency.

19   *Ripples*: another brand of crisps. They are, as it

happens, also produced by Tayto. They are crinkle-cut and would ordinarily cost more than the regular Tayto crisps.

22   *a batter*: a battering, a beating.

23   *The lake*: strictly speaking, there is no lake in Leenane; rather there is a large fjord knows as Killary harbour.

24   *be a schoolgirl*: just as the word 'my' is sometimes pronounced 'me' in this play, here we see the word 'by' being pronounced 'be'.

27   *humping a dead policeman*: 'humping' is used to mean 'carrying' here.

27   *shall we be having gas mark ten*: gas mark ten is the highest possible setting on a gas oven. The word 'shall' is rarely used in Ireland, and appears nowhere else in McDonagh's Irish plays. Coleman's use of this word, together with the phrase 'd'you know?' suggests that he is putting on a cultivated or 'posh' accent.

29   *Rotting in hell now, Tom Hanlon is*: in Catholic doctrine (as in many other religions), suicide is regarded as a sin so severe as to condemn the person who committed it to hell. In recent years, however, the Catholic Church has tended to adopt what it sees as a more compassionate view of suicide, suggesting that people who take their own lives due to mental illness are not fully aware of their actions and therefore have not committed a sin. Father Welsh shows here that he does not fully understand his own Church's doctrines – again revealing his inadequacies as a priest. On the other hand, his belief that people who commit suicide will go to hell makes his own death seem both more heroic and more tragic.

30   *Alias Smith and Jones*: an American television serial which ran for three seasons, premiering in 1971. One of its lead actors, Pete Duel, was found dead at his home in December 1971, having apparently shot himself.

30   *So long as you're sorry after you can still get into heaven*: Welsh again shows that his understanding of Catholic doctrine is slightly superficial. In the sacrament of confession, a

person who has committed a sin may be absolved – but only if he or she is sincerely repentant. Welsh's suggestion that someone can simply kill two dozen people, say sorry, and gain entry to heaven shows a limited understanding of his Church's attitude to contrition.

30 *Thou shouldst share and share alike the Bible says*: in fact, this phrase does not appear in the Bible.

33 *Scalectrix*: also known as 'scalextric', this is an electric car-racing game. Players use a hand-held control to direct electrified cars around a plastic track.

36 *lube*: perhaps an Anglicisation of the Gaelic word *lúbaire*, meaning a 'rogue', or the word *lúbán*, meaning 'a mistake'. In either case, Coleman is trying to convey his belief that Father Welsh in unhinged and mildly dangerous. The word 'lube' is not widely used in Ireland.

37 *Holland knocked us out of the fecking World Cup*: in the 1994 Football World Cup, which was held in the USA, Ireland played Holland in the last sixteen, losing 2–0.

37 *Packie fecking Bonner*: the goalkeeper for the Republic of Ireland between 1980 and 1996. Bonner was regarded as a skilled goalkeeper and made many memorable saves. In the match against Holland referred to above, he was badly at fault for one of the Dutch goals, however, allowing a rather simple shot to spill from his hands into the goal.

37 *high-horse*: on a high horse, affecting an air of superiority.

38 *letereen*: another use of the suffix '*–een*', here meaning 'little letter'.

39 *skittering*: the word 'skitter' is a colloquialism for excrement. Here, Welsh means that Girleen is throwing her money away as if it's nothing more than shit.

39 *Carraroe*: a coastal village in County Galway, about fifty kilometres from Leenane. Carraroe is part of the Gaeltacht, one of the Irish-speaking regions of Ireland.

39 *Freeman's catalogue*: Freeman's is a UK-based company

selling clothes and jewellery by mail order, though most of its business now is conducted online. Customers would choose their products from a catalogue, which was also usually distributed by post. Given Leenane's isolation, this is one of the easiest ways for Girleen to 'buy a few nice things'.

40   *Roderick*: Welsh's hesitation probably arises from fear of being laughed at. The name Roderick is very rare in Ireland and, unless shortened to Roddy, would be regarded as rather pretentious.

41   *slapeen*: 'a little slap'. The use of '-een' here softens the word, which suggests that Girleen is being flirtatious.

42   *Guinness*: a famous Irish stout.

42   *famine times*: although there were numerous famines in Ireland, right up to the end of the nineteenth century, the phrase 'famine times' most likely refers to the Great Famine of 1845 to 1848. In that famine, roughly one million Irish people died of starvation, while another million emigrated, mostly to Britain and north America. There is a strong sense in which Irish culture has subsequently been 'haunted' by the famine, as is evident from Girleen's references to ghosts.

43   *packed full of condoms*: in any conversation between a man and a woman, this reference to sex could be construed as flirtatious – and it's probably intended as such here. But Girleen is also breaking a taboo. The Catholic Church regards the use of contraception as a sin, with the result that condoms were not freely available for sale in Ireland until 1985. Father Welsh is therefore embarrassed twice here: firstly by the reference to sex and secondly by a joke about an object that his Church regards as inherently immoral.

44   *the Tribune*: the *Connaught Tribune* is a highly respected Galway newspaper, which features reports of local sporting events, such as the one referred to here.

45   *Yeres*: another unusual use of the word 'ye' by Father Welsh. Here he means 'yours' – specifically 'your house'.

45   *Gasur*: the word 'gasur' is an Irish-English word meaning 'boy'. It is possibly derived from the French 'garçon'.

45   *arging*: a mispronunciation of the word 'arguing'.

46   *listeen*: 'little list'.

47   *St Martin*: Valene is probably referring to Saint Martin de Porres, a sixteenth-century Peruvian saint who is often represented in statues as being black. St Martin was famed for his work with the poor. Interestingly, among the miracles attributed to him is the power of levitation – something that places the earlier discussion (on p. 18) about 'levitating darkies' in an interesting context.

48   *St Josephine's*: another Catholic girls' school, presumably somewhere in Connaught.

49   *Take a Break*: another women's magazine, also imported into Ireland from the UK. It is rather similar in content to *Woman's Own*, though it adopts a somewhat lighter tone occasionally.

49   *Bosnia*: formerly a region of Yugoslavia, Bosnia was the site of a vicious civil war that lasted from 1992 to 1995.

50   *Bella*: yet another UK-based women's magazine.

50   *Honey Nut Loops*: a breakfast cereal, produced by Kellog's. Since 2008, they have been known only as 'Honey Loops'.

51   *skitter*: see note to p. 39.

56   *feasteen*: 'lovely little feast'.

60   *Lettermullen*: a small island off the coast of County Galway.

61   *Claddagh Palace*: a cinema in Galway city (approximately sixty-five kilometres from Leenane). It had been demolished by the time the play premiered.

61   *Ker-Plunk*: a children's game. Players pull straws from a plastic container, upon which a number of marbles rest. Each time a straw is removed, there is a possibility that one of the marbles may fall (creating the 'kerplunk' noise). The winner is whichever player lets fewest marbles fall. The point here is that without the marbles, it is impossible to play the game.

62   *Spider Man*: Spider-man is a superhero whose
     adventures are serialised by Marvel Comics. One of his
     most dangerous enemies is Doctor Octopus, an evil
     scientist who moves around on four metallic legs that
     resemble the tentacles of an octopus.

62   *Pato Dooley*: a character from *The Beauty Queen of Leenane*.
     Pato has a brief love-affair with Maureen, and writes a
     letter inviting her to leave Ireland with him. Their
     chance of happiness together is destroyed when Mag
     burns this letter before Maureen has a chance to read
     it. This description of Pato contrasts with his
     presentation in *Beauty Queen*, in which he appears to be
     a gentle and sensitive man. The fact that his violence
     was provoked by a negative comment about his dead
     mother points to a strength of feeling that might explain
     why he is at first quite respectful towards Mag in that
     play.

63   *Ten years this has been going on*: this line is sometimes used
     to suggest that the play takes place in 1993. Yet we
     know that the action must take place after the 1994
     World Cup, so it seems best to assume that when
     Coleman uses the phrase 'ten years', he is speaking
     approximately. The action appears to take place in late
     1995.

64   *boss-eyes*: usually used to refer to a person with a squint
     or a lazy eye, or someone who is cross-eyed.

65   *brookeen*: 'the little brook'.

66   *Peneen*: 'the little pen'. Here the diminutive is being used
     sarcastically – Coleman is trying to provoke his brother.

Questions for Further Study

1. In *The Lonesome West*, Valene and Coleman appear to hate each other. Why, then, do they continue to live with each other?
2. Some critics have suggested that *The Lonesome West* is an anti-Catholic play. Yet in many ways Father Welsh is one of McDonagh's most sympathetic characters. Is McDonagh attacking religion, either through the characterisation of Welsh, or in some other way? And if not, how should we think about his treatment of that subject?
3. How may we understand Girleen's love for Father Welsh? Is it a teenage crush, of no real consequence? Is she attracted to him because she knows that she can't have him? How does McDonagh use her feelings in the play?
4. *The Lonesome West* has sometimes been seen as illustrating the maxim that 'hell is other people'. Do you think that phrase is appropriate to an understanding of the play?
5. Valene and Coleman claim that fighting 'does show you care'. Is their violence really a form of 'caring'? Do they really intend to harm each other when they fight?
6. Some critics suggest that *The Lonesome West* is an entirely amoral play – mainly because the characters who behave worst seem to thrive, while those who are admirable seem only to suffer. Does the play have a moral outlook and, if so, what is it?
7. *The Lonesome West* clearly has a lot to say about the problem of clerical child abuse in Ireland. Does it have any relevance for other countries or other religions?
8. At the end of the play, the lights linger on the crucifix, Father Welsh's letter and Girleen's chain. What does this image convey to you?

9. Examine McDonagh's use of Hiberno-English in the play. Do you think his use of language makes the play difficult to understand? Does that language have any other impact on audiences?

10. *The Lonesome West* is certainly a very funny play – yet it features two suicides and makes reference to countless other atrocities. What is the relationship between laughter and tragedy in this play?

11. It is clear that *The Lonesome West* features many negative images of the Irish. How would you respond to those critics who say that McDonagh is attempting to exploit anti-Irish prejudice?

12. Most of the play's action happens in one room, with many of the significant events (including all of the deaths) occurring offstage. Consider this contrast between the events that are shown and the events that audiences must instead imagine. What is the purpose of that contrast?

13. In the play's fifth scene, Father Welsh recites a letter that he has written. How would you as director, performer or designer present this scene without disrupting the audience's sense of the realism of the piece?

14. As an actor, how would you portray the character of Father Welsh? Do you think the audience is meant to find him sympathetic or foolish – or both?

15. Garry Hynes has stated that *The Lonesome West* should be performed in a style of heightened naturalism – that the actors must believe every line they deliver. Do you agree with this view? How would you advise your actors to present their characters, as a director of the play?

16. It has often been stated that the appearance of gun in a play's first scene means that someone will be shot before its conclusion. McDonagh doesn't quite fulfil that maxim, though the gun does go off. How does the constant threat of violence in the play affect the audience?

17. Many productions of *The Lonesome West* present the

scene in colours that are muted and drab. Do you think such lighting and set design is appropriate? How would you choose to present it?

18. In *The Lonesome West*, matters of life and death are discussed alongside apparently banal subjects, such as the merits of different brands of crisps. As director of the play, how would you achieve a balance between the play's substantial features and its more trivial elements?

19. How would you direct the actors playing Valene and Coleman? There is certainly a need to choreograph the brothers' fighting carefully. But is there also a need to point out resemblances or contrasts between the pair? And as an actor, how would you prepare yourself to play one of these roles?

20. A production of *The Lonesome West* involves the destruction of a stove and dozens of statuettes in every performance. As designer or producer of such a show, how would you seek to manage the repeated destruction of so many stage props?

21. *The Lonesome West* has sometimes been played as a straightforward comedy. Would you choose to perform it in this way? Are there other aspects of the play that you would want to bring out – and, if so, how would you go about doing so?

PATRICK LONERGAN lectures at National University of Ireland, Galway. His first book, *Theatre and Globalization: Irish Drama in the Celtic Tiger Era*, won the 2008 Theatre Book Prize. He has published widely on Irish theatre, including the Methuen Drama student edition of *The Lieutenant of Inishmore*, and is the director of the Synge Summer School.

Methuen Drama Student Editions

Jean Anouilh *Antigone* • John Arden *Serjeant Musgrave's Dance*
Alan Ayckbourn *Confusions* • Aphra Behn *The Rover* • Edward Bond
Lear • *Saved* • Bertolt Brecht *The Caucasian Chalk Circle* • *Fear and
Misery in the Third Reich* • *The Good Person of Szechwan* • *Life of Galileo* •
Mother Courage and her Children• *The Resistible Rise of Arturo Ui* • *The
Threepenny Opera* • Anton Chekhov *The Cherry Orchard* • *The Seagull* •
Three Sisters • *Uncle Vanya* • Caryl Churchill *Serious Money* • *Top Girls*
• Shelagh Delaney *A Taste of Honey* • Euripides *Elektra* • *Medea*•
Dario Fo *Accidental Death of an Anarchist* • Michael Frayn *Copenhagen*
• John Galsworthy *Strife* • Nikolai Gogol *The Government Inspector* •
Robert Holman *Across Oka* • Henrik Ibsen *A Doll's House* • *Ghosts*•
Hedda Gabler • Charlotte Keatley *My Mother Said I Never Should* •
Bernard Kops *Dreams of Anne Frank* • Federico García Lorca *Blood
Wedding* • *Doña Rosita the Spinster* (bilingual edition) •*The House of
Bernarda Alba* • (bilingual edition) • *Yerma* (bilingual edition) • David
Mamet *Glengarry Glen Ross* • *Oleanna* • Patrick Marber *Closer* • John
Marston *Malcontent* • Martin McDonagh *The Lieutenant of Inishmore* •
Joe Orton *Loot* • Luigi Pirandello *Six Characters in Search of an Author*
• Mark Ravenhill *Shopping and F***ing* • Willy Russell *Blood Brothers*
• *Educating Rita* • Sophocles *Antigone* • *Oedipus the King* • Wole
Soyinka *Death and the King's Horseman* • Shelagh Stephenson *The
Memory of Water* • August Strindberg *Miss Julie* • J. M. Synge *The
Playboy of the Western World* • Theatre Workshop *Oh What a Lovely
War* Timberlake Wertenbaker *Our Country's Good* • Arnold Wesker
The Merchant • Oscar Wilde *The Importance of Being Earnest* •
Tennessee Williams *A Streetcar Named Desire* • *The Glass Menagerie*

Methuen Drama Modern Classics

Jean Anouilh *Antigone* • Brendan Behan *The Hostage* • Robert Bolt
A Man for All Seasons • Edward Bond *Saved* • Bertolt Brecht *The
Caucasian Chalk Circle* • *Fear and Misery in the Third Reich* • *The Good
Person of Szechwan* • *Life of Galileo* • *The Messingkauf Dialogues* •
Mother Courage and Her Children • *Mr Puntila and His Man Matti* •
The Resistible Rise of Arturo Ui • *Rise and Fall of the City of
Mahagonny* • *The Threepenny Opera* • Jim Cartwright *Road* • *Two &
Bed* • Caryl Churchill *Serious Money* • *Top Girls* • Noël Coward
Blithe Spirit • *Hay Fever* • *Present Laughter* • *Private Lives* • *The Vortex* •
Shelagh Delaney *A Taste of Honey* • Dario Fo *Accidental Death of an
Anarchist* • Michael Frayn *Copenhagen* • Lorraine Hansberry *A
Raisin in the Sun* • Jonathan Harvey *Beautiful Thing* • David Mamet
Glengarry Glen Ross • *Oleanna* • *Speed-the-Plow* • Patrick Marber
Closer • *Dealer's Choice* • Arthur Miller *Broken Glass* • Percy Mtwa,
Mbongeni Ngema, Barney Simon *Woza Albert!* • Joe Orton
Entertaining Mr Sloane • *Loot* • *What the Butler Saw* • Mark Ravenhill
*Shopping and F***ing* • Willy Russell *Blood Brothers* • *Educating Rita* •
Stags and Hens • *Our Day Out* • Jean-Paul Sartre *Crime Passionnel* •
Wole Soyinka • *Death and the King's Horseman* • Theatre Workshop
Oh, What a Lovely War • Frank Wedekind • *Spring Awakening* •
Timberlake Wertenbaker *Our Country's Good*

Methuen Drama Modern Plays

include work by

Edward Albee
Jean Anouilh
John Arden
Margaretta D'Arcy
Peter Barnes
Sebastian Barry
Brendan Behan
Dermot Bolger
Edward Bond
Bertolt Brecht
Howard Brenton
Anthony Burgess
Simon Burke
Jim Cartwright
Caryl Churchill
Complicite
Noël Coward
Lucinda Coxon
Sarah Daniels
Nick Darke
Nick Dear
Shelagh Delaney
David Edgar
David Eldridge
Dario Fo
Michael Frayn
John Godber
Paul Godfrey
David Greig
John Guare
Peter Handke
David Harrower
Jonathan Harvey
Iain Heggie
Declan Hughes
Terry Johnson
Sarah Kane
Charlotte Keatley
Barrie Keeffe

Howard Korder
Robert Lepage
Doug Lucie
Martin McDonagh
John McGrath
Terrence McNally
David Mamet
Patrick Marber
Arthur Miller
Mtwa, Ngema & Simon
Tom Murphy
Phyllis Nagy
Peter Nichols
Sean O'Brien
Joseph O'Connor
Joe Orton
Louise Page
Joe Penhall
Luigi Pirandello
Stephen Poliakoff
Franca Rame
Mark Ravenhill
Philip Ridley
Reginald Rose
Willy Russell
Jean-Paul Sartre
Sam Shepard
Wole Soyinka
Simon Stephens
Shelagh Stephenson
Peter Straughan
C. P. Taylor
Theatre Workshop
Sue Townsend
Judy Upton
Timberlake Wertenbaker
Roy Williams
Snoo Wilson
Victoria Wood

Methuen Drama Contemporary Dramatists
include

John Arden (two volumes)
Arden & D'Arcy
Peter Barnes (three volumes)
Sebastian Barry
Dermot Bolger
Edward Bond (eight volumes)
Howard Brenton
  (two volumes)
Richard Cameron
Jim Cartwright
Caryl Churchill (two volumes)
Sarah Daniels (two volumes)
Nick Darke
David Edgar (three volumes)
David Eldridge
Ben Elton
Dario Fo (two volumes)
Michael Frayn (three volumes)
David Greig
John Godber (four volumes)
Paul Godfrey
John Guare
Lee Hall (two volumes)
Peter Handke
Jonathan Harvey
  (two volumes)
Declan Hughes
Terry Johnson (three volumes)
Sarah Kane
Barrie Keeffe
Bernard-Marie Koltès
  (two volumes)
Franz Xaver Kroetz
David Lan
Bryony Lavery
Deborah Levy
Doug Lucie

David Mamet (four volumes)
Martin McDonagh
Duncan McLean
Anthony Minghella
  (two volumes)
Tom Murphy (six volumes)
Phyllis Nagy
Anthony Neilsen (two volumes)
Philip Osment
Gary Owen
Louise Page
Stewart Parker (two volumes)
Joe Penhall (two volumes)
Stephen Poliakoff
  (three volumes)
David Rabe (two volumes)
Mark Ravenhill (two volumes)
Christina Reid
Philip Ridley
Willy Russell
Eric-Emmanuel Schmitt
Ntozake Shange
Sam Shepard (two volumes)
Wole Soyinka (two volumes)
Simon Stephens (two volumes)
Shelagh Stephenson
David Storey (three volumes)
Sue Townsend
Judy Upton
Michel Vinaver
  (two volumes)
Arnold Wesker (two volumes)
Michael Wilcox
Roy Williams (three volumes)
Snoo Wilson (two volumes)
David Wood (two volumes)
Victoria Wood

Methuen Drama World Classics

include

Jean Anouilh (two volumes)
Brendan Behan
Aphra Behn
Bertolt Brecht (eight volumes)
Büchner
Bulgakov
Calderón
Čapek
Anton Chekhov
Noël Coward (eight volumes)
Feydeau (two volumes)
Eduardo De Filippo
Max Frisch
John Galsworthy
Gogol
Gorky (two volumes)
Harley Granville Barker
  (two volumes)
Victor Hugo
Henrik Ibsen (six volumes)
Jarry

Lorca (three volumes)
Marivaux
Mustapha Matura
David Mercer (two volumes)
Arthur Miller (six volumes)
Molière
Musset
Peter Nichols (two volumes)
Joe Orton
A. W. Pinero
Luigi Pirandello
Terence Rattigan
  (two volumes)
W. Somerset Maugham
  (two volumes)
August Strindberg
  (three volumes)
J. M. Synge
Ramón del Valle-Inclán
Frank Wedekind
Oscar Wilde

Methuen Drama Classical Greek Dramatists

Aeschylus Plays: One
(Persians, Seven Against Thebes, Suppliants,
Prometheus Bound)

Aeschylus Plays: Two
(Oresteia: Agamemnon, Libation-Bearers, Eumenides)

Aristophanes Plays: One
(Acharnians, Knights, Peace, Lysistrata)

Aristophanes Plays: Two
(Wasps, Clouds, Birds, Festival Time, Frogs)

Aristophanes & Menander: New Comedy
(Women in Power, Wealth, The Malcontent,
The Woman from Samos)

Euripides Plays: One
(Medea, The Phoenician Women, Bacchae)

Euripides Plays: Two
(Hecuba, The Women of Troy, Iphigeneia at Aulis,
Cyclops)

Euripides Plays: Three
(Alkestis, Helen, Ion)

Euripides Plays: Four
(Elektra, Orestes, Iphigeneia in Tauris)

Euripides Plays: Five
(Andromache, Herakles' Children, Herakles)

Euripides Plays: Six
(Hippolytos, Suppliants, Rhesos)

Sophocles Plays: One
(Oedipus the King, Oedipus at Colonus, Antigone)

Sophocles Plays: Two
(Ajax, Women of Trachis, Electra, Philoctetes)

For a complete catalogue
of Methuen Drama titles
write to:

Methuen Drama
Bloomsbury Publishing Plc
50 Bedford Square
London WC1B 3DP

or you can visit our website at:

www.methuendrama.com